BUSINESS MANAGEMENT

IN THE

LOCAL CHURCH

REVISED AND EXPANDED

DAVID R. POLLOCK

FOREWORD BY

LARRY BURKETT

MOODY PRESS

CHICAGO

Contents

List of Forms and Illustrations

Foreword

For many years I have been dismayed by the lack of good, biblical information on church financial administration. With his expanded *Business Management in the Local Church*, Dave Pollock has stepped in and "filled the gap." This manual is packed with practical —and profoundly useful—guidelines for the management of church finances.

Whenever Dave has appeared on our radio program *Money Matters*, I've been amazed at the wisdom he has been able to apply in the often volatile arena of the stewardship of church funds. I can heartily recommend this book to pastors, administrators, and laymen alike, and I am pleased that the tremendous needs our churches face with regard to church financial administration have at last been expertly addressed.

LARRY BURKETT
CHRISTIAN FINANCIAL CONCEPTS

Introduction

The management of resources within the local church is rapidly becoming one of the more significant challenges facing church leaders today. Operating churches in an organized, efficient, and effective manner isn't nearly as simple as it once was. That is because of growing public awareness, increased governmental scrutiny, and the recognition on the part of church leaders in general that improvements in managing church finances must be made.

The basic mission of the church today has not changed from that of the first-century body of believers—it is to evangelize, equip, and care for the flock. A major difference, however, is the type—and use—of the physical resources placed at our disposal to accomplish that task.

The operation of a church is, in many respects, quite similar to that of a business. Even though the local church is not in business to make a profit, it is still a business—the Lord's business. Therefore, to have the respect of the community in which it serves, and thus an effective testimony, it is essential that churches use good business methods. The apostle Paul's statement in 1 Corinthians 14:40, "All things must be done properly and in an orderly manner," certainly applies to the temporal aspects of a church as well as to its worship procedures.

Chapter 1

Sharpening the Vision of the Local Church

You're trying to run the church like a corporation" was the objection heard when it was suggested that the church form a Long-Range Planning Committee. In the past, concerns were often voiced about the loss of flexibility or spontaneity when formal goal-setting procedures were proposed. But, whereas the concept of strategic planning may once have been considered a luxury that only large ministries could afford to be involved in, today it is a necessity for all churches—large or small.

A recent survey[1] showed that in the area of short-range planning 92 percent of large churches (five hundred or more members) had one-year plans, whereas 77 percent of the smaller churches polled had a formal, written, twelve-month strategy. However, when the question of long-range (three to five year) planning was asked, the figures plunged to 42 percent for the large and 14 percent for the small churches.

Two primary arguments are often raised against strategic planning and budgeting: unforeseen changes in the economy, and overcontrol.

Objections to Long-Range Planning

Changing Economic Conditions

Changes in the economy in the form of recessions, inflation, and rising interest rates all can affect the church collection plate. The impact is especially felt when economic conditions cause a decrease in giving. For instance, a church located in a suburban community could experience a drop in contributions if home mortgage interest rates were to increase. Those families on variable mortgage rates would have less spendable income.

1. R. Henry Migloire, Oral Roberts University, Tulsa, Oklahoma (1986).

The issue here isn't whether it is right or wrong for people to cut back on their giving. The point is that there could be less money available to carry out some of the church's plans. It is important, therefore, to develop within the budgeting process both positive and negative scenarios. With the introduction of computerized, electronic spreadsheets, the "what ifs" of budgeting can be reduced to hard-copy black-and-white.

Therefore, a 10 percent increase in giving or a 7 percent reduction, for instance, can be calculated selectively or across the board to all budgeted departments. The affects of increased or decreased giving could be applied to any or all ministries of the church, from one month to one decade. A changing economy doesn't mean that planning can't go forward and be effective.

Overcontrol

The second objection to long-range planning is that it could place a choke hold on creativity or flexibility. This argument can be valid in many cases—not right, but valid. Often the budget becomes chiseled in stone, and new opportunities get shot down because "they're not in the budget."

I'm not advocating throwing financial projections out the window or "busting" the budget with overspending. However, there is no reason line-items can't be moved around or projects with a lesser priority set aside in the interest of a new opportunity. Flexibility is the key to overcoming this drawback to strategic planning.

Long-range planning is the blueprint of the church's future, showing where the church expects to be after a given period of time. This blueprint is usually in the form of a game plan, complete with projections of income, personnel, space, facility requirements, and other significant factors that affect church growth. These long-range projections are based on past performance and assumptions about the future and are normally projected three to five years into the future.

It should be understood that budgeting is a result of long-range planning and should fall in behind the strategic plan—not come before it. First comes the plan, then comes the identification of needed resources.

Five Characteristics of Long-Range Plans

1. *Identification*—Long-term goals are identified by asking "Where does the church want to go?"
2. *Potential*—Church leadership is alerted to the potential opportunities and risks before they occur, thus allowing the church to take advantage of the opportunities and avoid the risks.

3. *Projections*—After goals are identified, the long-range plan projects future financial requirements, people needs, and other resource necessities.

4. *Alternatives*—Alternative courses of action can be formulated to reach the goals. Each course of action should be evaluated. This begins the process of selecting those alternatives that are most feasible in light of the church's resources.

5. *Review*—Long-range planning provides a framework for periodic review so that a church can measure its progress and, when necessary, make modifications.

"It is important to remember that long-range planning is, to a large extent, based on short-term planning. Any long-range planning not based on the church's current functional plan is an exercise in futility. Conversely, to maximize results and prevent leaders and staff from going in all directions, functional plans must be integrated into one, unified, long-range plan."[2]

Since planning deals with the unknown, once again it should be emphasized that a strategic plan needs to be *flexible*. And although a long-range plan cannot guarantee success, it can certainly help a church bring current problems under control, overcome future obstacles, and maximize its potential for effectiveness.

2. *Strategic Planning* (Monterey, Calif.: Business Research & Communications, 1986), 8.

Section 1

Church and Law

Chapter 2

What the Government Requires of Your Church

Christ established it, He died for it, and He promised us that the very gates of hell could not conquer it. For the believer, that is a well-known, comforting, and unmistakable fact. Secular society, on the other hand, has different ideas about the church. Without question, the true biblical church has often been the subject of scorn and persecution, and sometimes it has simply been ignored.

So far the North American church has not had to endure many of the hardships experienced by others throughout history. Perhaps our day is coming. In fact, there *are* signs that our secular society is losing its tolerance for the church. Federal, state, and local laws are being passed that continue to restrict and, in some instances, inhibit the activities of local churches.

Church leaders need to be aware of how they are viewed in the eyes of the law in order to avoid problems and complications with the "system." The days of cloaking church activities under the protective mantle of the First Amendment or other constitutional interpretations of freedom of religion are disappearing. Therefore, within the context of society's changing perceptions, how should the church position itself in today's legal and legislative environment?

Generally speaking—and for our purposes—a church by definition has two meanings. First, there is the physical description: "a building set apart or consecrated for public worship." Then there is the people-oriented designation: "a group of worshipers: a congregation."[3]

A legal definition could also encompass both of these definitions. When a group of worshipers who call themselves a church wish to officially establish themselves as a "church," two choices face them right away: Should a church be a nonprofit corpora-

3. *Webster's New World Dictionary*, 2d ed. (New York: Simon & Schuster, 1980).

21

tion or an unincorporated association? Legally, a church is not required to become incorporated. However, certain advantages are available to the members if they do choose to incorporate.

Incorporation

The main advantages of incorporation are liability protection and tax exemption. A church that chooses to do business as a corporation has protection from liability. Members are exempt from liability if the leaders or other members engage in any wrongful activity. In the event of a legal judgment against the church, claims would be paid out of an insurance policy or from the assets of the church—but not from assets of the members. If an individual officer or person is guilty of wrongdoing, a lawsuit could be brought against that individual, but the remaining members would be free from liability.

The disadvantages of not incorporating are significant. Although some churches refuse to become "entangled" in governmental regulations on philosophical grounds, perhaps they should reconsider their decision. On a practical level, it is difficult to do business without incorporating. Banks are reluctant to open accounts without someone taking ultimate responsibility, which usually means the senior pastor. A church functioning as an unincorporated association normally places the pastor or one or more trustees at risk for all debts, contracts, and legal matters. Furthermore, while an unincorporated church cannot sue or be sued, in most states legal action can be brought against the church members.

Governmental Benefits of Incorporating

When a church incorporates, it normally secures a nonprofit status. The benefits of a nonprofit distinction are many. Federal statutes provide certain direct benefits to nonprofit corporations.

- A nonprofit may apply and receive exemption from federal income taxes.
- In some instances, a nonprofit may receive a reduced postal rate.

On a state level, nonprofits enjoy certain other benefits:

- Exemption from state income taxes
- Release from paying franchise taxes
- Exemption from property taxes
- Exemption from sales tax

When applying for nonprofit, tax-exempt status under federal law, churches usually must receive a nonprofit status from their state government. Once this is accomplished, a church would apply for the status of a public charity and the designation as a "501 (c)(3)" organization. This 501 (c)(3) classification affects both the activities that the organization may engage in and the manner in which contributions will be treated.

The Internal Revenue Code defines and sets forth guidelines and qualifications for a nonprofit corporation. These include the drafting of Articles of Incorporation and By-laws. These documents lay out the legal structure of the church government along with certain limitations on activities. It is advisable either to secure the services of an attorney when preparing these documents or to thoroughly research the preparation of the text at a local library. Generally speaking, to secure the 501 (c)(3) status from the federal government, your Articles of Incorporation must include the following:

1. A "Religious Purpose" clause
2. A clause that states that there will be no "Propaganda or Political Activity"
3. A method for disbanding the corporation or a "Provision for Dissolution Clause"

Once the church has satisfactorily met all the government's requirements, a letter of determination will be issued from the IRS confirming the 501 (c)(3) status.

It is interesting to note that a church is not required to incorporate in order to gain tax-exempt status from the federal government. However, the issues of protection from liability and other corporate benefits should be considered. There are churches that have chosen not to file for 501 (c)(3) status on theological grounds. The primary disadvantage of not being considered a 501 (c)(3) exempt organization is that, if a contributor should be audited by the IRS in connection with his or her charitable donations, the church might, on behalf of the donor, be required to prove that it substantially meets the IRS criteria. Once a church goes through this process a few times, it might wish to reconsider its objection to federal recognition.

Receipting Requirements

In January 1994 new rules went into effect that place requirements on churches in the area of providing receipts to contributors. The Budget Reconciliation Act of 1993 set forth two new guidelines regarding substantiation of contributions and deductible disclosure.

Substantiation of Contributions

Church contributors may no longer rely on canceled checks as proof that they made donations. The IRS now requires that donors who claim tax deductions for gifts of

$250 or more must ask their church to provide them with a receipt of their contributions. The $250 figure refers to the amount of each gift, not to the total amount given to a nonprofit organization over the course of a year. If the church elects to file a report of all gifts of more than $250 with the IRS, the donor does not need a receipt. However, I am not aware of any churches that are providing that service. Nevertheless, the church should take the initiative in providing individual donors with receipts instead of waiting for donors to request them.

The best procedure for churches is to keep track of individual contributions throughout the year. Then, as do most churches, provide an itemized listing of all donations at the end of the calendar year. The acknowledgment by the church can be in the form of a letter, a postcard (not advisable for the sake of privacy), or a report produced by a computer. Many church donor software programs designed especially for this purpose are available in a wide range of prices. Churches may also design their own report format by using a spreadsheet program. It is recommended that these reports be prepared and sent out quarterly, not just at year's end. Remember that there must be separate entries on these reports for gifts of $250 or more. The receipting report should cover giving to all funds, not only the general fund.

Deductible Disclosure

Another rule that went into effect in January 1994 deals with revealing what portion of a contribution of more than $75 covers the price of a premium—a meal, a book, or other item of value. The church is required to tell the donor that only the amount of the gift that does not go toward the cost of the premium is deductible. For instance, if the church solicits a gift of $100, and the donor receives a leather-bound, commemorative book with a value of $30, the church must state the true value of the contribution as $70 ($100 – $30 = $70). Although this might seem like a lot of trouble, it is a requirement, and many charities have already been doing this for several years because they saw the rule coming. And, remember, this law applies to nontangible items as well. (There goes the "charitable" cruise!)

The value placed on the premium and communicated to the donor must be a good-faith estimate. The best method is to print the information on the ticket, appeal letter, or other printed matter involved. Notice that this rule applies to gifts of more than $75, not $250, as in the substantiation rule discussed above.

These new rules were not designed to single out churches and to make things more difficult for them. They are actually the result of abuses by many charities in general, not churches per se. Churches in the United States enjoy unique privileges in regard to their tax-exempt status. The government still believes that the local church makes a positive contribution to its community and society in general. But privileges also carry responsibilities, and here are two new ones.

24

Reporting Requirements

Though some of the reporting requirements will be touched on briefly in this section, each church should use a competent CPA who is well acquainted with tax laws as they relate specifically to churches. This cannot be stressed strongly enough.

County

It may be necessary to comply with county or local property tax laws if you have been exempted from property tax. This is normally done on an annual basis.

State

Many states require churches to file a form on an annual basis informing them of the names of the church's officers as well as the individual to contact for legal purposes. This is often done through the State Corporation Commission or Secretary of State. Other requirements for churches could involve Workman's Compensation Insurance. However, in most states the church is exempt from paying unemployment taxes. Moreover, state disability taxes vary in different states. There may be additional forms to file if your employees are subject to state (also city and county) income taxes.

Federal

If the church is an employer, it is subject to state and federal labor, withholding, and other tax laws. Compliance is required—not an option—and protection as a "church" is not assured. Church financial leaders need to be familiar with several forms that relate to the area of taxation.

IRS Form 8274	This deals with social security tax for church employers. (See Exhibit 2–1.)
IRS Form 4361	This form relates to Social Security and ministers. (See Exhibit 2–2.)
IRS Form 941 or 941SS	These forms are for the reporting of city, state, or federal tax withholding. If the church is exempt from Social Security, 941SS is to be submitted. (See Exhibits 2–3, 2–4.)
IRS Form W-4	The W-4 form pertains to all employees and some minister employees. (See Exhibit 2–5.)
IRS Form W-2	This form is a statement of earnings. (See Exhibit 2–6.)

IRS Form W-3	This is sent to the Social Security Administration and, in some instances, to the state. (See Exhibit 2–7.)
IRS Form 1099 MISC.	This form is issued to self-employed individuals. (See Exhibit 2–8.)
IRS Form 1099 INT.	This is issued to anyone to whom the church paid interest of more than $10 in a calendar year. (See Exhibit 2–9.)
IRS Form 1096	This is a transmittal form for all 1099 forms. The church should determine state requirements. (See Exhibit 2–10.)
IRS Form 5578	Every 501 (c)(3) organization operating a private school must file this form annually. (See Exhibit 2–11.)
IRS Form 8283	This form is submitted to the IRS for donations of noncash items in excess of $500 or less than $5,000. Read it carefully. (See Exhibit 2–12.)
IRS Form 8282	This is to be completed by the church only if noncash items are sold. (See Exhibit 2–13.)
IRS Form 8300	If a church (or any other ministry) receives $10,000 or more in cash in any business or trade transaction (e.g., rental of property or a parking lot), it would need to be reported on Form 8300. (See Exhibit 2–14.)
IRS Form W-9	This form needs to be completed by a visiting ministry or other independent contractor in the event a Form 1099 should be required for these people at a later date. (See Exhibit 2–15.)
IRS Form I-9	The Immigration and Naturalization Service requires this to be on file for every employee. (See Exhibit 2–16.)
IRS Form 990	A church is not obligated to fill out and return this form. (See Exhibit 2–17.)
IRS Form 990T	A church that receives $1,000 or more in gross income from an unrelated trade or business must file this form. (See Exhibit 2–18.)

IRS Form 1040ES	This form is to be filled out by ministers on a quarterly basis for their estimated federal income and SECA taxes.[4] (See Exhibit 2–19.)

Churches should seek the advice of a qualified CPA in these matters, since most of these forms require further in-depth understanding. There may also be additional requirements if a church employs a number of people who are engaged in trade or commerce, or are doing business in other states.

Privileges with Accountability

Although it may seem that the government places a lot of burdensome rules and regulations on churches, it should all be kept in perspective. On balance, no other nation in the world provides as many benefits and exemptions for religious organizations as does the United States. Sometimes we forget some of the freedoms granted to our churches.

Christ certainly recognized the distinction between political and spiritual responsibilities when He said, "Give to Caesar what is Caesar's, and to God what is God's" (Matthew 22:21 NIV*). As long as the laws do not inhibit clear and unmistakable biblical teaching regarding the mission and mandate of the local church, churches need to cooperate with the government and obey the rules.

4. Don L. Buckel and Barbara E. Buckel, *The Church Administration "How To" Manual* (Lakeside, Calif.: Administrative Assistance), 1990, chap. 8, p. 7.
  *New International Version.

Exhibit 2–1

Form **8274** (Rev. September 1994) Department of the Treasury Internal Revenue Service	**Certification by Churches and Qualified Church-Controlled Organizations Electing Exemption From Employer Social Security and Medicare Taxes**	**File Two Copies**

Please type or print

Full name of organization	Employer identification number
Address (number and street or P.O. box number if mail is not delivered to street address)	
City, state, and ZIP code	Date wages first paid
If exemption is based on a group ruling, give full name of central organization	Group exemption number

Sign Here

I certify that the above named organization is a church or qualified church-controlled organization which, as defined in section 3121(w) of the Internal Revenue Code, is opposed for religious reasons to the payment of employer social security and Medicare taxes, and elects not to be subject to such taxes.

▶ _____
(Signature of authorized official)　　(Title)　　(Date)

X40121 01-17-9

Exhibit 2–2

Form 4361
(Rev. February 1994)
Department of the Treasury
Internal Revenue Service

Application for Exemption From Self-Employment Tax for Use by Ministers, Members of Religious Orders and Christian Science Practitioners

OMB No. 1545-0168
Expires 2-28-97

File Original and Two Copies

File original and two copies and attach supporting documents. This exemption is granted only if the IRS returns a copy to you marked "approved."

Please type or print	**1**	**Social security number**
		Telephone number (optional)

2 Check ONE box:
☐ Christian Science practitioner
☐ Member of religious order not under a vow of poverty
☐ Ordained minister, priest, rabbi
☐ Commissioned or licensed minister (see line 6)

3 Date ordained, licensed, etc. (Attach supporting document.)

4 Legal name of ordaining, licensing, or commissioning body or religious order

Address

Employer identification no.

5 Enter the first 2 years, after the date shown on line 3, that you had net self-employment earnings of $400 or more, any of which came from services as a minister, priest, rabbi, etc.; member of a religious order; or Christian Science practitioner ▶ 19____ 19____

6 If you apply for the exemption as a licensed or commissioned minister, and your denomination also ordains ministers, please indicate how your ecclesiastical powers differ from those of an ordained minister of your denomination. Attach a copy of your denomination's by-laws relating to the powers of ordained, commissioned, or licensed ministers.

7 I certify that I am conscientiously opposed to, or because of my religious principles I am opposed to, the acceptance (for services I perform as a minister, member of a religious order not under a vow of poverty, or a Christian Science practitioner) of any public insurance that makes payments in the event of death, disability, old age, or retirement; or that makes payments toward the cost of, or provides services for, medical care. (Public insurance includes insurance systems established by the Social Security Act.)

I certify that as a duly ordained, commissioned, or licensed minister of a church or a member of a religious order not under a vow of poverty, I have informed the ordaining, commissioning, or licensing body of my church or order that I am conscientiously opposed to, or because of religious principles, I am opposed to the acceptance (for services I perform as a minister or as a member of a relgious order) of any public insurance that makes payments in the event of death, disability, old age, or retirement; or that makes payments toward the cost of, or provides services for, medical care, including the benefits of any insurance system established by the Social Security Act.

I certify that I did not file an effective waiver certificate (Form 2031) electing social security coverage on earnings as a minister, member of a religious order not under a vow of poverty, or a Christian Science practitioner.

I request to be exempted from paying self-employment tax on my earnings from services as a minister, member of a religious order not under a vow of poverty, or a Christian Science practitioner, under section 1402(e) of the Internal Revenue Code. I understand that the exemption, if granted, will apply only to these earnings. Under penalties of perjury, I declare that I have examined this application and to the best of my knowledge and belief, it is true and correct.

Signature ▶   Date ▶

Caution: Form 4361 is **not proof** of the right to an exemption from Federal income tax withholding or social security tax, the right to a parsonage allowance exclusion (section 107), assignment by your religious superiors to a particular job, or the exemption or church status of the ordaining, licensing, commissioning body, or religious order.

For Internal Revenue Service Use

☐ Approved for exemption from self-employment tax on ministerial earnings
☐ Disapproved for exemption from self-employment tax on ministerial earnings

By _____   _____
         (Director's signature)   (Date)

D40053 10-24-9

Exhibit 2–3

Form **941**
(Rev. January 1995)

Department of the Treasury
Internal Revenue Service

4141

Employer's Quarterly Federal Tax Return

► See separate instructions for information on completing this return.
Please type or print.

OMB No. 1545-0029

Enter state code for state in which deposits made . ► (see page 3 of instructions).

Name (as distinguished from trade name)

Trade name, if any

Address (number and street)

Date quarter ended

Employer identification number

City, state, and ZIP code

| T |
| FF |
| FD |
| FP |
| I |
| T |

If address is different from prior return, check here ►

IRS Use

1 1 1 1 1 1 1 1 1 1   2   3 3 3 3 3   4 4 4

5 5 5   6   7   8 8 8 8 8   9 9 9   10 10 10 10 10 10 10 10 10 10

If you do not have to file returns in the future, check here .... ► ☐   and enter date final wages paid ►

If you are a seasonal employer, see **Seasonal employers** on page 1 of the instructions and check here .... ► ☐

1 Number of employees (except household) employed in the pay period that includes March 12th .... ►

2	Total wages and tips, plus other compensation	2	
3	Total income tax withheld from wages, tips, and sick pay	3	
4	Adjustment of withheld income tax for preceding quarters of calendar year	4	
5	Adjusted total of income tax withheld (line 3 as adjusted by line 4)	5	

6a	Taxable social security wages	$	X 12.4% (.124) =	6a	
b	Taxable social security tips	$	X 12.4% (.124) =	6b	
7	Taxable Medicare wages and tips	$	X 2.9% (.029) =	7	

8 Total social security and Medicare taxes (add lines 6a, 6b, and 7). Check here if wages are not subject to social security and/or Medicare tax .... ► ☐ | 8 | |

9 Adjustment of social security and Medicare taxes (see instructions for required explanation)
Sick Pay $ _____ + Fractions of Cents $ _____ + Other $ _____ = | 9 | |

10 Adjusted total of social security and Medicare taxes (line 8 as adjusted by line 9) .... | 10 | |

11 **Total taxes** (add lines 5 and 10) .... | 11 | |

12 Advance earned income credit (EIC) payments made to employees, if any .... | 12 | |

13 Net taxes (subtract line 12 from line 11. **This should equal line 17, column (d) below** (or line D of Schedule B (Form 941)) .... | 13 | |

14 Total deposits for quarter, including overpayment applied from a prior quarter .... | 14 | |

15 **Balance due** (subtract line 14 from line 13). Pay to Internal Revenue Service .... | 15 | |

16 Overpayment, if line 14 is more than line 13, enter excess here ► $ _____
and check if to be: ☐ Applied to next return   **OR**   ☐ Refunded.

● **All filers:** If line 13 is less than $500, you need not complete line 17 or Schedule B.
● **Semiweekly depositors:** Complete Schedule B and check here .... ► ☐
● **Monthly depositors:** Complete line 17, columns (a) through (d), and check here .... ► ☐

17	**Monthly Summary of Federal Tax Liability.**		
(a) First month liability	**(b)** Second month liability	**(c)** Third month liability	**(d)** Total liability for quarter

Sign Here

Under penalties of perjury, I declare that I have examined this return, including accompanying schedules and statements, and to the best of my knowledge and belief, it is true, correct, and complete.

Signature ►

Print Your Name and Title ►

Date ►

For Paperwork Reduction Act Notice, see page 1 of separate instructions.

Form **941** (Rev. 1-95)

B40051 03-12-95

30

Exhibit 2–4

Form **941-SS**

(Rev. January 1995)
Department of the Treasury
Internal Revenue Service

Employer's Quarterly Federal Tax Return

American Samoa, Guam, the Commonwealth of the Northern Mariana Islands,
and the U.S. Virgin Islands

▶ See Circular SS for more information concerning employment tax returns.

OMB No. 1545-0029

T	
FF	
FD	
FP	
I	
T	

Name (as distinguished from trade name)

Date quarter ended

Trade name, if any

Employer identification number

Address (number and street)

City, state, and ZIP code

IRS Use

1 1 1 1 1 1 1 1 1 1   2   3 3 3 3 3 3   4 4 4

5 5 5   6   7   8 8 8 8 8   9 9 9   10 10 10 10 10 10 10 10 10 10

If address is
different from
prior return,
check here ▶ ☐

If you do not have to file returns in the future, check here ▶ ☐   and enter date final wages paid .... ▶

If you are a seasonal employer, see **Seasonal Employers** on page 2 and check here .... ▶ ☐

Complete for First Quarter Only

1	Number of employees (except household) employed in the pay period that includes March 12th	1

2-5

6a	Taxable social security wages	$	X 12.4% (.124) =	6a
b	Taxable social security tips	$	X 12.4% (.124) =	6b
7	Taxable Medicare wages and tips	$	X 2.9% (.029) =	7
8	Taxable social security and Medicare taxes (add lines 6a, 6b, and 7)			8
9	Adjustment of social security and Medicare taxes (see instructions for required explanation)			
	Sick Pay $ _____ + Fractions of Cents $ _____ + Other $ _____ =			9
10	Adjusted total of social security and Medicare taxes (line 8 as adjusted by line 9 – see instructions). **This should equal line 17, col. (d), below or line D of Schedule B (Form 941)**			10

11-13

14	Total deposits for quarter, including overpayment applied from prior quarter, from your records	14
15	**Balance due** (subtract line 14 from line 10). Pay to Internal Revenue Service	15
16	Overpayment, if line 14 is more than line 10, enter excess here ▶ $ _____ and check if to be:	
	☐ Applied to next return, or ☐ Refunded.	

- **All filers:** If line 10 is less than $500, you need not complete line 17 or Schedule B (Form 941).
- **Semiweekly depositors:** Complete Schedule B (Form 941) and check here .... ▶ ☐
- **Monthly depositors:** Complete line 17, columns (a) through (d), and check here .... ▶ ☐

17 **Monthly Summary of Federal Tax Liability.**

(a) First month liability	(b) Second month liability	(c) Third month liability	(d) Total liability for quarter

Under penalties of perjury, I declare that I have examined this return, including accompanying schedules and statements, and to the best of my knowledge and belief, it is true, correct, and complete.

Print Your Name
and Title ▶

Signature ▶

Date ▶

For Paperwork Reduction Act Notice, see page 2.

Form **941-SS** (Rev. 1-95)

B40059 01-19-95

31

Exhibit 2–5

Form W-4 (1995)

Want More Money In Your Paycheck?

If you expect to be able to take the earned income credit for 1995 and a child lives with you, you may be able to have part of the credit added to your take-home pay. For details, get Form W-5 from your employer.

Purpose. Complete Form W-4 so that your employer can withhold the correct amount of Federal income tax from your pay.
Exemption from Withholding. Read line 7 of the certificate below to see if you can claim exempt status. If exempt, complete line 7; but do not complete lines 5 and 6. No Federal income tax will be withheld from your pay. Your exemption is good for 1 year only. It expires February 15, 1996.
Note: You cannot claim exemption from withholding if (1) your income exceeds $650 and includes unearned income (e.g., interest

and dividends), and (2) another person can claim you as a dependent on their tax return.
Basic Instructions. Employees who are not exempt should complete the Personal Allowances Worksheet. Additional worksheets are provided on page 2 for employees to adjust their withholding allowances based on itemized deductions, adjustments to income, or two-earner/two-job situations. Complete all worksheets that apply to your situation. The worksheets will help you figure the number of withholding allowances you are entitled to claim. However, you may claim fewer allowances than this.
Head of Household. Generally, you may claim head of household filing status on your tax return only if you are unmarried and pay more than 50% of the costs of keeping up a home for yourself and your dependent(s) or other qualifying individuals.
Nonwage Income. If you have a large amount of nonwage income, such as interest or

dividends, you should consider making estimated tax payments using Form 1040-ES. Otherwise, you may find that you owe additional tax at the end of the year.
Two Earners/Two Jobs. If you have a working spouse or more than one job, figure the total number of allowances you are entitled to claim on all jobs using worksheets from only one Form W-4. This total should be divided among all jobs. Your withholding will usually be most accurate when all allowances are claimed on the W-4 filed for the highest paying job and zero allowances are claimed for the others.
Check Your Withholding. After your W-4 takes effect, you can use **Pub. 919,** Is My Withholding Correct for 1995?, to see how the dollar amount you are having withheld compares to your estimated total annual tax. We recommend you get Pub. 919 especially if you used the Two Earner/Two Job Worksheet and your earnings exceed $150,000 (Single) or $200,000 (Married). Call 1-800-829-3676 to order Pub. 919. Check your telephone directory for the IRS assistance number for further help.

Personal Allowances Worksheet

A Enter "1" for **yourself** if no one else can claim you as a dependent .... **A** _____

B Enter "1" if:
- You are single and have only one job; or
- You are married, have only one job, and your spouse does not work; or
- Your wages from a second job or your spouse's wages (or the total of both) are $1,000 or less.

.... **B** _____

C Enter "1" for your **spouse.** But, you may choose to enter -0- if you are married and have either a working spouse or more than one job (this may help you avoid having too little tax withheld) .... **C** _____

D Enter number of **dependents** (other than your spouse or yourself) you will claim on your tax return .... **D** _____

E Enter "1" if you will file as **head of household** on your tax return (see conditions under **Head of Household** above) .... **E** _____

F Enter "1" if you have at least $1,500 of **child or dependent care expenses** for which you plan to claim a credit .... **F** _____

G Add lines A through F and enter total here. **Note:** This amount may be different from the number of exemptions you claim on your return ...... ▶ **G** _____

For accuracy, do all work-sheets that apply.
- If you plan to **itemize or claim adjustments to income** and want to reduce your withholding, see the Deductions and Adjustments Worksheet on page 2.
- If you are **single** and have more than one job and your combined earnings from all jobs exceed $30,000 OR if you are **married** and have a **working spouse or more than one job,** and the combined earnings from all jobs exceed $50,000, see the Two-Earner/Two-Job Worksheet on page 2 if you want to avoid having too little tax withheld.
- If **neither** of the above situations applies, **stop here** and enter the number from line G on line 5 of Form W-4 below.

– – – – – – – – – – – – – – **Cut here and give the certificate to your employer. Keep the top portion for your records.** – – – – – – – – – – – – – –

Form **W-4**	**Employee's Withholding Allowance Certificate**	OMB No. 1545-0010
Department of the Treasury Internal Revenue Service	▶ For Privacy Act and Paperwork Reduction Act Notice, see page 2.	**1995**

1 _____

2 Your social security number _____

3 ☐ Single ☐ Married ☐ Married, but withhold at higher Single rate.
Note: If married, but legally separated, or spouse is a nonresident alien, check the Single box.

4 If your last name differs from that on your social security card, check here and call 1-800-772-1213 for a new card ... ▶ ☐

5 Total number of allowances you are claiming (from line G above or from the worksheets on page 2 if they apply) .... **5** _____

6 Additional amount, if any, you want withheld from each paycheck .... **6** $ _____

7 I claim exemption from withholding for 1995 and I certify that I meet BOTH of the following conditions for exemption:
- Last year I had a right to a refund of **ALL** Federal income tax withheld because I had **NO** tax liability; **AND**
- This year I expect a refund of **ALL** Federal income tax withheld because I expect to have **NO** tax liability.

If you meet both conditions, enter "EXEMPT" here .... ▶ **7** _____

Under penalties of perjury, I certify that I am entitled to the number of withholding allowances claimed on this certificate or entitled to claim exempt status.

Employee's signature ▶ _____ Date ▶ _____, 19 ___

8 Employer's name and address (Employer: Complete 8 and 10 only if sending to the IRS)

9 Office code (optional)

10 Employer identification number

B40147 12-05-94

Exhibit 2–6

a Control number	22222	Void ☐	For Official Use Only ► OMB No. 1545-0008	
b Employer's identification number			**1** Wages, tips, other compensation	**2** Federal income tax withheld
c Employer's name, address, and ZIP code			**3** Social security wages	**4** Social security tax withheld
			5 Medicare wages and tips	**6** Medicare tax withheld
			7 Social security tips	**8** Allocated tips
d Employee's social security number			**9** Advance EIC payment	**10** Dependent care benefits
e Employee's name (first, middle initial, last)			**11** Nonqualified plans	**12** Benefits included in box 1
			13 See Instrs. for box 13	**14** Other

	15 Statutory employee ☐	Deceased ☐	Pension plan ☐	Legal rep. ☐	942 emp. ☐	Subtotal ☐	Deferred compensation ☐
f Employee's address and ZIP code							

16 State	Employer's state I.D. No.	**17** State wages, tips, etc.	**18** State income tax	**19** Locality name	**20** Local wages, tips, etc.	**21** Local income tax

Cat. No. 10134D   Department of the Treasury—Internal Revenue Service

Form W-2 Wage and Tax Statement **1994**

For Paperwork Reduction Act Notice, see separate instructions.

Copy A For Social Security Administration

Do NOT Cut or Separate Forms on This Page

33

Exhibit 2–7

DO NOT STAPLE

a Control number	33333	For Official Use Only ▶ OMB No. 1545-0008		

b **Kind of Payer** ▶	941 ☐ Military ☐ 943 ☐	1 Wages, tips, other compensation	2 Federal income tax withheld
	CT-1 ☐ 942 ☐ Medicare govt. emp. ☐	3 Social security wages	4 Social security tax withheld
c Total number of statements	d Establishment number	5 Medicare wages and tips	6 Medicare tax withheld
e Employer's identification number		7 Social security tips	8 Allocated tips
f Employer's name		9 Advance EIC payments	10 Dependent care benefits
		11 Nonqualified plans	12 Deferred compensation
		13 Adjusted total social security wages and tips	
		14 Adjusted total Medicare wages and tips	
g Employer's address and ZIP code			
h Other EIN used this year		15 Income tax withheld by third-party payer	
i Employer's state I.D. No.			

OCR Form Do NOT Photocopy

Under penalties of perjury, I declare that I have examined this return and accompanying documents, and, to the best of my knowledge and belief, they are true, correct, and complete.

Signature ▶ _____   Title ▶ _____   Date ▶ _____

Telephone number (____) _____

Form **W-3** Transmittal of Wage and Tax Statements **1994**   Department of the Treasury Internal Revenue Service

---

Paperwork Reduction Act Notice

We ask for the information on this form to carry out the Internal Revenue laws of the United States. You are required to give us the information. We need it to ensure that you are complying with these laws and to allow us to figure and collect the right amount of tax.

The time needed to complete and file this form will vary depending on individual circumstances. The estimated average time is 27 minutes. If you have comments concerning the accuracy of this time estimate or suggestions for making this form more simple, we would be happy to hear from you. You can write to both the **Internal Revenue Service,** Attention: Reports Clearance Officer, PC:FP, Washington, DC 20224; and the **Office of Management and Budget,** Paperwork Reduction Project (1545-0008), Washington, DC 20503. Do NOT send the form to either of these offices. Instead, see **Where To File.**

Note: *Extra postage may be necessary if the report you send contains more than a few pages or if the envelope is larger than letter size.*

Items To Note

Change To Filing Address.—Beginning with 1994 tax year, all Forms W-2 and W-3 (including forms for household employees) should be sent to the Social Security Administration's Wilkes-Barre Data Operations Center. See **Where To File** for the complete address.

Change to Kind of Payer Box.—The 941/941E box was retitled 941 because **Form 941E,** Quarterly Return of Withheld Federal Income Tax and Medicare Tax, is obsolete for payments made after December 31, 1993.

Change to Form.—The size of boxes c, d, and e changed.

Information Reporting Call Site.—The IRS operates a centralized call site to answer questions about reporting on Forms W-3, W-2, 1099, and other information returns. If you have questions related to reporting on information returns, you may call (304) 263-8700 (not a toll-free number).

Where To File

Please send this entire page with Copy A of Forms W-2 to the Social Security Administration (SSA) at the following address:

Social Security Administration
Data Operations Center
Wilkes-Barre, PA   18769

General Instructions

Purpose of Form.—Use this form to transmit Copy A of Form W-2. Keep page 2 (Your Copy) and Copy D of Form W-2 for your records.

Cat. No. 10159Y

34

Exhibit 2–8

☐ CORRECTED (if checked)

PAYER'S name, street address, city, state, and ZIP code		**1 Rents** $	OMB No. 1545-0115	
		2 Royalties $	**1994**	**Miscellaneous Income**
		3 Prizes, awards, etc. $		
PAYER'S Federal identification no.	RECIPIENT'S identification no.	**4 Federal income tax withheld** $	**5 Fishing boat proceeds** $	
RECIPIENT'S name, street address, city, state, and ZIP code		**6 Medical and health care payments** $	**7 Nonemployee compensation** $	**Copy 2** **To be filed**
		8 Substitute payments in lieu of dividends or interest $	**9 Payer made direct sales of $5,000 or more of consumer products to a buyer (recipient) for resale** ▶ ☐	**with** **recipient's** **state income**
		10 Crop insurance proceeds $	**11 State income tax withheld** $	**tax return,** **when**
Account number (optional)		**12 State/Payer's state number**		**required.**

Form **1099-MISC**   Department of the Treasury–Internal Revenue Service

---

☐ CORRECTED (if checked)

PAYER'S name, street address, city, state, and ZIP code		**1 Rents** $	OMB No. 1545-0115	
		2 Royalties $	**1994**	**Miscellaneous Income**
		3 Prizes, awards, etc. $		
PAYER'S Federal identification no.	RECIPIENT'S identification no.	**4 Federal income tax withheld** $	**5 Fishing boat proceeds** $	
RECIPIENT'S name, street address, city, state, and ZIP code		**6 Medical and health care payments** $	**7 Nonemployee compensation** $	**Copy 2** **To be filed**
		8 Substitute payments in lieu of dividends or interest $	**9 Payer made direct sales of $5,000 or more of consumer products to a buyer (recipient) for resale** ▶ ☐	**with** **recipient's** **state income**
		10 Crop insurance proceeds $	**11 State income tax withheld** $	**tax return,** **when**
Account number (optional)		**12 State/Payer's state number**		**required.**

Form **1099-MISC**   Department of the Treasury–Internal Revenue Service

---

☐ CORRECTED (if checked)

PAYER'S name, street address, city, state, and ZIP code		**1 Rents** $	OMB No. 1545-0115	
		2 Royalties $	**1994**	**Miscellaneous Income**
		3 Prizes, awards, etc. $		
PAYER'S Federal identification no.	RECIPIENT'S identification no.	**4 Federal income tax withheld** $	**5 Fishing boat proceeds** $	
RECIPIENT'S name, street address, city, state, and ZIP code		**6 Medical and health care payments** $	**7 Nonemployee compensation** $	**Copy 2** **To be filed**
		8 Substitute payments in lieu of dividends or interest $	**9 Payer made direct sales of $5,000 or more of consumer products to a buyer (recipient) for resale** ▶ ☐	**with** **recipient's** **state income**
		10 Crop insurance proceeds $	**11 State income tax withheld** $	**tax return,** **when**
Account number (optional)		**12 State/Payer's state number**		**required.**

Form **1099-MISC**   Department of the Treasury–Internal Revenue Service

B40085 03-03-95   **NF**

Exhibit 2–9

☐ CORRECTED (if checked)

PAYER'S name, street address, city, state, and ZIP code	Payer's RTN (optional)	OMB No. 1545-0112	
		1994	**Interest Income**

PAYER'S Federal identification no.	RECIPIENT'S identification no.	1 Interest income not included in box 3 $		**Copy B**
RECIPIENT'S name, street address, city, state, and ZIP code		2 Early withdrawal penalty $	3 Interest on U.S. Savings Bonds and Treas. obligations $	**For Recipient** This is important tax information & is being furnished to the Internal Revenue Service. If you are required to file a return, a negligence penalty or other sanction may be imposed on you if this income is taxable and the IRS determines that it has not been reported.
		4 Federal income tax withheld $		
		5 Foreign tax paid	6 Foreign country or U.S. possession	
Account number (optional)		$		

Form **1099-INT** (Keep for your records) Department of the Treasury – Internal Revenue Service

- **CUT HERE** -

☐ CORRECTED (if checked)

PAYER'S name, street address, city, state, and ZIP code	Payer's RTN (optional)	OMB No. 1545-0112	
		1994	**Interest Income**

PAYER'S Federal identification no.	RECIPIENT'S identification no.	1 Interest income not included in box 3 $		**Copy B**
RECIPIENT'S name, street address, city, state, and ZIP code		2 Early withdrawal penalty $	3 Interest on U.S. Savings Bonds and Treas. obligations $	**For Recipient** This is important tax information & is being furnished to the Internal Revenue Service. If you are required to file a return, a negligence penalty or other sanction may be imposed on you if this income is taxable and the IRS determines that it has not been reported.
		4 Federal income tax withheld $		
		5 Foreign tax paid	6 Foreign country or U.S. possession	
Account number (optional)		$		

Form **1099-INT** (Keep for your records) Department of the Treasury – Internal Revenue Service

- **CUT HERE** -

☐ CORRECTED (if checked)

PAYER'S name, street address, city, state, and ZIP code	Payer's RTN (optional)	OMB No. 1545-0112	
		1994	**Interest Income**

PAYER'S Federal identification no.	RECIPIENT'S identification no.	1 Interest income not included in box 3 $		**Copy B**
RECIPIENT'S name, street address, city, state, and ZIP code		2 Early withdrawal penalty $	3 Interest on U.S. Savings Bonds and Treas. obligations $	**For Recipient** This is important tax information & is being furnished to the Internal Revenue Service. If you are required to file a return, a negligence penalty or other sanction may be imposed on you if this income is taxable and the IRS determines that it has not been reported.
		4 Federal income tax withheld $		
		5 Foreign tax paid	6 Foreign country or U.S. possession	
Account number (optional)		$		

Form **1099-INT** (Keep for your records) Department of the Treasury – Internal Revenue Service

NF

36

Exhibit 2–10

DO NOT STAPLE   6969

| Form **1096**
Department of the Treasury
Internal Revenue Service | **Annual Summary and Transmittal of U.S. Information Returns** | OMB No. 1545-0108
1994 |

ATTACH IRS LABEL HERE

| If you are not using a preprinted label, enter in box 1 or 2 below the identification number you used as the filer on the information returns being transmitted. Do not fill in both boxes 1 and 2. | Name of person to contact if IRS needs more information

Telephone number | **For Official Use Only** |

| **1** Employer identification number | **2** Social security number | **3** Total number of forms | **4** Federal income tax withheld
$ | **5** Total amount reported with this Form 1096
$ |

Enter an "X" in only one box below to indicate the type of form being filed.   If this is your FINAL return, enter an "X" here .... ▶ ☐

W-2G	1098	1099-A	1099-B	1099-C	1099-DIV	1099-G	1099-INT	1099-MISC	1099-OID	1099-PATR	1099-R	1099-S	5498
32	81	80	79	85	91	86	92	95	96	97	98	75	28

Please return this entire page to the Internal Revenue Service. Photocopies are NOT acceptable.

Under penalties of perjury, I declare that I have examined this return and accompanying documents, and, to the best of my knowledge and belief, they are true, correct, and complete.

Signature ▶ _____ Title ▶ _____ Date ▶ _____

Instructions

Purpose of Form. – Use this form to transmit paper Forms 1099, 1098, 5498, and W-2G to the Internal Revenue Service. DO NOT USE FORM 1096 TO TRANSMIT MAGNETIC MEDIA. See **Form 4804**, Transmittal of Information Returns Reported Magnetically/Electronically.

Use of Preprinted Label. – If you received a preprinted label from the IRS with Package 1099, place the label in the name and address area of this form inside the brackets. Make any necessary changes to your name and address on the label. However, do not use the label if the taxpayer identification number (TIN) shown is incorrect. **Do not prepare your own label. Use only the IRS-prepared label that came with your Package 1099.**

If you are not using a preprinted label, enter the filer's name, address (including room, suite, or other unit number), and TIN in the spaces provided on the form.

Filer. – **The name, address, and TIN of the filer on this form must be the same as those you enter in the upper left area of Form 1099, 1098, 5498, or W-2G.** A filer includes a payer, a recipient of mortgage interest payments (including points), a broker, a barter exchange, a creditor, a person reporting real estate transactions, a trustee or issuer of an individual retirement arrangement (including an IRA or SEP), and a lender who acquires an interest in secured property or who has reason to know that the property has been abandoned.

Transmitting to the IRS. – Send the forms in a flat mailing (not folded). Group the forms by form number and transmit each group with **a separate** Form 1096. For example, if you must file both Forms 1098 and 1099-A, complete one Form 1096 to transmit your Forms 1098 and another Form 1096 to transmit your Forms 1099-A. You need not submit original and corrected returns separately.

Box 1 or 2. – Complete only if you are not using a preprinted IRS label. Individuals not in a trade or business must enter their social security number in box 2; sole proprietors and all others must enter their employer identification number in box 1. However, sole proprietors who do not have an employer identification number must enter their social security number in box 2.

Box 3. – Enter the number of forms you are transmitting with this Form 1096. Do not include blank or voided forms or the Form 1096 in your total. Enter the number of correctly completed forms, not the number of pages, being transmitted. For example, if you send one page of three-to-a-page Forms 5498 with a Form 1096 and you have correctly completed two Forms 5498 on that page, enter "2" in box 3 of Form 1096.

Box 4. – Enter the total Federal income tax withheld shown on the forms being transmitted with this Form 1096.

Box 5. – No entry is required if you are filing Form 1099-A or 1099-G. For all other forms, enter the total of the amounts from the specific boxes of the forms listed below:

Form W-2G	Box 1
Form 1098	Boxes 1 and 2
Form 1099-B	Boxes 2 and 3
Form 1099-C	Box 2
Form 1099-DIV	Boxes 1a, 5, and 6
Form 1099-INT	Boxes 1 and 3
Form 1099-MISC	Boxes 1, 2, 3, 5, 6, 7, 8, and 10
Form 1099-OID	Boxes 1 and 2
Form 1099-PATR	Boxes 1, 2, 3, and 5
Form 1099-R	Box 1
Form 1099-S	Box 2
Form 5498	Boxes 1 and 2

For more information and the Paperwork Reduction Act Notice, see the Instructions for Forms 1099, 1098, 5498, and W-2G.

NF
Form **1096** (1994)

B40001 03-03-95

Exhibit 2–11

Form **5578** (Rev. February 1993) Department of the Treasury Internal Revenue Service	Annual Certification of Racial Nondiscrimination for a Private School Exempt from Federal Income Tax (For use by organizations that do not file Form 990 or 990-EZ)	OMB No. 1545-0213 Expires 1-31-96 For IRS ▶ use ONLY

For the period beginning _____ , 19 ___ , and ending _____ , 19 ___

1a	Name of organization that operates, supervises, and/or controls school(s)	1b	Employer identification number

Address (number and street or P.O. box no. if mail is not delivered to street address) | Room/suite

City or town, state, and ZIP code

2a	Name of central organization holding group exemption letter covering the school(s). (If same as 1a above, write "Same" and complete 2c.) If the organization in 1a above holds an individual exemption letter, write "Not Applicable."	2b	Employer identification number

Address (number and street or P.O. box no. if mail is not delivered to street address) | 2c | Group exemption number (see instructions under Definitions)

City or town, state, and ZIP code | Room/suite

3a	Name of school (if more than one school, write "See Attached," and attach list of the names, addresses, ZIP codes, and employer identification numbers of the schools). If same as 1a above, write "Same"	3b	Employer identification number, if any

Address (number and street or P.O. box no. if mail is not delivered to street address) | Room/suite

City or town, state, and ZIP code

Under penalties of perjury, I hereby certify that I am authorized to take official action on behalf of the above school(s) and that to the best of my knowledge and belief the school(s) has (have) satisfied the applicable requirements of section 4.01 through 4.05 of Revenue Procedure 75-50 for the period covered by this certification.

_____ (Signature)   _____ (Title or authority of signer)   _____ (Date)

X40109 02-15-9

For Paperwork Reduction Act Notice, see instr.

Exhibit 2–12

Form **8283**	**Noncash Charitable Contributions**	OMB No. 1545-0908 Expires 11-30-95
(Rev. November 1992) Department of the Treasury Internal Revenue Service	▶ Attach to your tax return if the total deduction claimed for all property contributed exceeds $500. ▶ See separate instructions.	Attachment Sequence No. **55**

Name(s) shown on your income tax return	Identifying number

Note: Figure the amount of your contribution deduction before completing this form. See your tax return instructions.

Section A—Include in this section **only** items (or groups of similar items) for which you claimed a deduction of $5,000 or less per item or group, and certain publicly traded securities (see instructions).

Part I Information on Donated Property—If you need more space, attach a statement.

1	(a) Name and address of the donee organization	(b) Description of donated property
A		
B		
C		
D		
E		

Note: If the amount you claimed as a deduction for an item is $500 or less, you do not have to complete columns (d), (e), and (f).

	(c) Date of the contribution	(d) Date acquired by donor (mo., yr.)	(e) How acquired by donor	(f) Donor's cost or adjusted basis	(g) Fair market value	(h) Method used to determine the fair market value
A						
B						
C						
D						
E						

Part II Other Information—If you gave less than an entire interest in property listed in Part I, complete lines 2a–2e. If restrictions were attached to a contribution listed in Part I, complete lines 3a–3c.

2 If less than the entire interest in the property is contributed during the year, complete the following:

a Enter letter from Part I that identifies the property _____. If Part II applies to more than one property, attach a separate statement.

b Total amount claimed as a deduction for the property listed in Part I: **(1)** For this tax year _____
   (2) For any prior tax years _____.

c Name and address of each organization to which any such contribution was made in a prior year (complete only if different than the donee organization above).

   Name of charitable organization (donee)

   Address (number, street, and room or suite no.)

   City or town, state, and ZIP code

d For tangible property, enter the place where the property is located or kept _____
e Name of any person, other than the donee organization, having actual possession of the property _____

3 If conditions were attached to any contribution listed in Part I, answer the following questions and attach the required statement (see instructions):

		Yes	No
a	Is there a restriction, either temporary or permanent, on the donee's right to use or dispose of the donated property?		
b	Did you give to anyone (other than the donee organization or another organization participating with the donee organization in cooperative fundraising) the right to the income from the donated property or to the possession of the property, including the right to vote donated securities, to acquire the property by purchase or otherwise, or to designate the person having such income, possession, or right to acquire?		
c	Is there a restriction limiting the donated property for a particular use?		

For Paperwork Reduction Act Notice, see separate instructions. Cat. No. 62299J Form **8283** (Rev. 11-92)

Exhibit 2–13

Form 8282

(Rev. Nov. 1992)
Department of the Treasury
Internal Revenue Service

Donee Information Return

(Sale, Exchange, or Other Disposition of Donated Property)

OMB No. 1545-0908
Expires 11-30-95

Give Copy to Donor

Please Print or Type	Name of Charitable organization (donee)	Employer identification number

Note: If you are the original donee, **DO NOT** complete Part II, or column (c) of Part III.

Part I Information on ORIGINAL DONOR and DONEE You gave the property to

1a Name of the original donor of the property	1b Identifying number

Note: Complete lines 2a–2d only if you gave this property to another charitable organization (successor donee).

2a Name of charitable organization	2b Employer identification number

2c Address (number, street, and room or suite number)

2d City or town, state, and ZIP code

Part II Information on PREVIOUS DONEES-Complete this part only if you were not the first donee to receive the property.

If you were the second donee, leave lines 4a–4d blank. If you were a third or later donee, complete lines 3a–4d.

On lines 4a–4d give information on the preceding donee (the one who gave you the property).

3a Name of original donee	3b Employer identification number

3c Address (number, street, and room or suite number)

3d City or town, state, and ZIP code

4a Name of preceding donee	4b Employer identification number

4c Address (number, street, and room or suite number)

4d City or town, state, and ZIP code

Part III Information on DONATED PROPERTY

(a) Description of donated property sold, exchanged, or otherwise disposed of (attach a separate sheet if more space is needed)	(b) Date you received the item(s)	(c) Date the first donee received the item(s) (if you weren't the first)	(d) Date item(s) sold, exchanged, or otherwise disposed of	(e) Amount received upon disposition

D40073 10-24-9

D193 For Paperwork Reduction Act Notice, see instr.

40

Exhibit 2–14

Form **8300**

(Rev. August 1994)

Department of the Treasury
Internal Revenue Service

**Report of Cash Payments Over $10,000
Received in a Trade or Business**

▶ See instructions for definition of cash.

Please type or print.

OMB No. 1545-0892

1 Check appropriate boxes if: **a** ☐ amends prior report; **b** ☐ suspicious transaction.

Part I **Identity of Individual From Whom the Cash Was Received**

2 If more than one individual is involved, see instructions and check here . . . . ▶ ☐

3 Last name	**4** First name	**5** M.I.	**6** Social security number

7 Address (number, street, and apt. or suite no.)	**8** Date of birth (see instructions)

9 City	**10** State	**11** ZIP code	**12** Country (if not U.S.)	**13** Occupation, profession, or business

14 Method used to verify identity: **a** Describe identification ▶ ....

b Issued by .... **c** Number

Part II **Person (See Definitions) on Whose Behalf This Transaction Was Conducted**

15 If this transaction was conducted on behalf of more than one person, see instructions and check here . . . . . ▶ ☐

16 Individual's last name or Organization's name	**17** First name	**18** M.I.	**19** Social security number

20 Doing business as (DBA) name (see instructions)

Employer identification number

21 Alien identification: **a** Describe identification ▶ ....

b Issued by .... **c** Number

22 Address (number, street, and apt. or suite no.)	**23** Occupation, profession, or business

24 City	**25** State	**26** ZIP code	**27** Country (if not U.S.)

Part III **Description of Transaction and Method of Payment**

28 Date cash received	**29** Total cash received	**30** If cash was received in more than one payment, check here . . . ▶ ☐	**31** Total price if different from item 29
	$ .00		$ .00

32 Amount of cash received (in U.S. dollar equivalent) (see instructions):

a U.S. currency $ _____ .00 (Amount in $100 bills or higher $ _____ .00)

b Foreign currency _____ .00 (Country ▶ _____)

c Cashier's check(s) _____ .00   Issuer's name(s) and serial number(s) of the monetary instrument(s) ▶ ....◀..

d Money order(s) _____ .00 ....

e Bank draft(s) _____ .00 ....

f Traveler's check(s) _____ .00

33 Type of transaction

a ☐ personal property purchased **f** ☐ debt obligations paid

b ☐ real property purchased **g** ☐ exchange of cash

c ☐ personal services provided **h** ☐ escrow or trust funds

d ☐ business services provided **i** ☐ other (specify) ▶

e ☐ intangible property purchased

34 Specific description of property or service shown in 33. (Give serial or registration number, address, etc.)

▶ ....

....

....

Part IV **Business That Received Cash**

35 Name of business that received cash	**36** Employer identification number
37 Address (number, street, and apt. or suite no.)	Social security number

38 City	**39** State	**40** ZIP code	**41** Nature of your business

42 Under penalties of perjury, I declare that to the best of my knowledge the information I have furnished above is true, correct, and complete.

**Sign
Here**

_____ _____ _____ ( )

(Authorized signature of business that received cash) (Title) (Date signed) (Telephone number of business)

Cat. No. 62133S Form **8300** (Rev. 8-94)

41

Exhibit 2–15

<table>
<tr>
<td>

Form W-9
(Rev. March 1994)
Department of the Treasury
Internal Revenue Service

</td>
<td>

**Request for Taxpayer
Identification Number and Certification**

</td>
<td>

**Give form to the
requester. Do NOT
send to the IRS.**

</td>
</tr>
</table>

Please print or type

Name (If joint names, list first and circle the name of the person or entity whose number you enter in Part I below. **See instructions on page 2 if your name has changed.**)

Business name (Sole proprietors see instructions on page 2.)

Please check appropriate box: ☐ Individual/Sole proprietor ☐ Corporation ☐ Partnership ☐ Other ▶ ....

Address (number, street, and apt. or suite no.)

Requester's name and address (optional)

City, state, and ZIP code

Part I — Taxpayer Identification Number (TIN)

Enter your TIN in the appropriate box. For individuals, this is your social security number (SSN). For sole proprietors, see the instructions on page 2. For other entities, it is your employer identification number (EIN). If you do not have a number, see **How To Get a TIN** below.

Note: *If the account is in more than one name, see the chart on page 2 for guidelines on whose number to enter.*

Social security number

OR

Employer identification number

List account number(s) here (optional)

Part II — For Payees Exempt From Backup Withholding (See Part II instructions on page 2)

▶

Part III — Certification

Under penalties of perjury, I certify that:

1. The number shown on this form is my correct taxpayer identification number (or I am waiting for a number to be issued to me), **and**

2. I am not subject to backup withholding because: **(a)** I am exempt from backup withholding, or **(b)** I have not been notified by the Internal Revenue Service that I am subject to backup withholding as a result of a failure to report all interest or dividends, or **(c)** the IRS has notified me that I am no longer subject to backup withholding.

Certification Instructions.—You must cross out item **2** above if you have been notified by the IRS that you are currently subject to backup withholding because of underreporting interest or dividends on your tax return. For real estate transactions, item **2** does not apply. For mortgage interest paid, the acquisition or abandonment of secured property, cancellation of debt, contributions to an individual retirement arrangement (IRA), and generally payments other than interest and dividends, you are not required to sign the Certification, but you must provide your correct TIN. (Also see **Part III instructions** on page 2.)

Sign Here   Signature ▶   Date ▶

Section references are to the Internal Revenue Code.

Purpose of Form.—A person who is required to file an information return with the IRS must get your correct TIN to report income paid to you, real estate transactions, mortgage interest you paid, the acquisition or abandonment of secured property, cancellation of debt, or contributions you made to an IRA. Use Form W-9 to give your correct TIN to the requester (the person requesting your TIN) and, when applicable, (1) to certify the TIN you are giving is correct (or you are waiting for a number to be issued), (2) to certify you are not subject to backup withholding, or (3) to claim exemption from backup withholding if you are an exempt payee. Giving your correct TIN and making the appropriate certifications will prevent certain payments from being subject to backup withholding.

Note: *If a requester gives you a form other than a W-9 to request your TIN, you must use the requester's form if it is substantially similar to this Form W-9.*

What Is Backup Withholding?—Persons making certain payments to you must withhold and pay to the IRS 31% of such payments under certain conditions. This is called "backup withholding." Payments that could be subject to backup withholding include interest, dividends, broker and barter exchange transactions, rents, royalties, nonemployee pay, and certain payments from fishing boat operators. Real estate transactions are not subject to backup withholding.

If you give the requester your correct TIN, make the proper certifications, and report all your taxable interest and dividends on your tax return, your payments will not be subject to backup withholding. Payments you receive will be subject to backup withholding if:

1. You do not furnish your TIN to the requester, or

2. The IRS tells the requester that you furnished an incorrect TIN, or

3. The IRS tells you that you are subject to backup withholding because you did not report all your interest and dividends on your tax return (for reportable interest and dividends only), or

4. You do not certify to the requester that you are not subject to backup withholding under 3 above (for reportable interest and dividend accounts opened after 1983 only), or

5. You do not certify your TIN. See the Part III instructions for exceptions

Certain payees and payments are exempt from backup withholding and information reporting. See the Part II instructions and the separate **Instructions for the Requester of Form W-9.**

How To Get a TIN.—If you do not have a TIN, apply for one immediately. To apply, get **Form SS-5**, Application for a Social Security Number Card (for individuals), from your local office of the Social Security Administration, or **Form SS-4**, Application for Employer Identification Number (for businesses and all other entities), from your local IRS office.

If you do not have a TIN, write "Applied For" in the space for the TIN in Part I, sign and date the form, and give it to the requester. Generally, you will then have 60 days to get a TIN and give it to the requester. If the requester does not receive your TIN within 60 days, backup withholding, if applicable, will begin and continue until you furnish your TIN.

Cat. No. 10231X

Form **W-9** (Rev. 3-94)

42

Exhibit 2–16

U. S. Department of Justice
Immigration and Naturalization Service

OMB No. 1115-0136
Employment Eligibility Verification

Please read instructions carefully before completing this form. The instructions must be available during completion of this form. **ANTI-DISCRIMINATION NOTICE. It is illegal to discriminate against work eligible individuals. Employers CANNOT specify which document(s) they will accept from an employee. The refusal to hire an individual because of a future expiration date may also constitute illegal discrimination.**

Section 1. Employee Information and Verification. To be completed and signed by employee at the time employment begins

Print Name: Last	First	Middle Initial	Maiden Name

Address (Street Name and Number)	Apt. #	Date of Birth (month/day/year)

City	State	Zip Code	Social Security #

I am aware that federal law provides for imprisonment and/or fines for false statements or use of false documents in connection with the completion of this form.

I attest, under penalty of perjury, that I am (check one of the following):
- [ ] A citizen or national of the United States
- [ ] A Lawful Permanent Resident (Alien # A _____)
- [ ] An alien authorized to work until _____
   (Alien # or Admission # _____)

Employee's Signature	Date (month/day/year)

Preparer and/or Translator Certification. (To be completed and signed if Section 1 is prepared by a person other than the employee.) I attest, under penalty of perjury, that I have assisted in the completion of this form and that to the best of my knowledge the information is true and correct.

Preparer's/Translator's Signature	Print Name

Address (Street Name and Number, City, State, Zip Code)	Date (month/day/year)

Section 2. Employer Review and Verification. To be completed and signed by employer. **Examine one document from List A OR examine one document from List B and one from List C** as listed on page 2 of this form and record the title, number and expiration date, if any, of the document(s)

	List A	OR	List B	AND	List C
Document title:	_____		_____		_____
Issuing authority:	_____		_____		_____
Document #:	_____		_____		_____
Expiration Date (if any):	_____		_____		_____
Document #:	_____				
Expiration Date (if any):	_____				

CERTIFICATION - I attest, under penalty of perjury, that I have examined the document(s) presented by the above-named employee, that the above-listed document(s) appear to be genuine and to relate to the employee named, that the employee began employment on (month/day/year) _____ and that to the best of my knowledge the employee is eligible to work in the United States. (State employment agencies may omit the date the employee began employment).

Signature of Employer or Authorized Representative	Print Name	Title

Business or Organization Name Address (Street Name and Number, City, State, ZIP Code)	Date (month/day/year)

Section 3. Updating and Reverification. To be completed and signed by employer

A. New Name (if applicable)	B. Date of rehire (month/day/year) (if applicable)

C. If employee's previous grant of work authorization has expired, provide the information below for the document that establishes current employment eligibility.

Document Title:	Document #:	Expiration Date (if any):

I attest, under penalty of perjury, that to the best of my knowledge, this employee is eligible to work in the United States, and if the employee presented document(s), the document(s) I have examined appear to be genuine and to relate to the individual.

Signature of Employer or Authorized Representative	Date (month/day/year)

Form I-9 (Rev. 11-21-91) N

B40106 02-03-9

Exhibit 2–17

Form **990**	**Return of Organization Exempt From Income Tax**	OMB No. 1545-0047
	Under section 501(c) of the Internal Revenue Code (except black lung benefit trust or private foundation) or section 4947(a)(1) nonexempt charitable trust	19**94**
Department of the Treasury Internal Revenue Service	Note: *The organization may have to use a copy of this return to satisfy state reporting requirements.*	This Form is Open to Public Inspection

A For the 1994 calendar year, OR tax year period beginning _____ , 1994, and ending _____ , 19___

B Check if:	Please use IRS label or print or type. See Specific Instruc- tions.	**C** Name of organization	**D** Employer identification number
☐ Change of address			
☐ Initial return		Number and street (or P.O. box if mail is not delivered to street address) Room/suite	**E** State registration number
☐ Final return			
☐ Amended return (required also for State reporting)		City, town, or post office, state, and ZIP code	**F** Check ► ☐ if exemption application is pending

G Type of organization—► ☐ Exempt under section 501(c)(   ) ◄ (insert number) OR ► ☐ section 4947(a)(1) nonexempt charitable trust

Note: *Section 501(c)(3) exempt organizations and 4947(a)(1) nonexempt charitable trusts MUST attach a completed Schedule A (Form 990).*

H(a) Is this a group return filed for affiliates? . . . . ☐ Yes ☐ No

(b) If "Yes," enter the number of affiliates for which this return is filed:. . ► _____

(c) Is this a separate return filed by an organization covered by a group ruling? ☐ Yes ☐ No

I If either box in H is checked "Yes," enter four-digit group exemption number (GEN) ► ....

J Accounting method: ☐ Cash ☐ Accrual ☐ Other (specify) ►

K Check here ► ☐ if the organization's gross receipts are normally not more than $25,000. The organization need not file a return with the IRS; but if it received a Form 990 Package in the mail, it should file a return without financial data. **Some states require a complete return.**

Note: *Form 990-EZ may be used by organizations with gross receipts less than $100,000 and total assets less than $250,000 at end of year.*

Part I Statement of Revenue, Expenses, and Changes in Net Assets or Fund Balances

Revenue

1	Contributions, gifts, grants, and similar amounts received:		
a	Direct public support	1a	
b	Indirect public support	1b	
c	Government contributions (grants)	1c	
d	**Total** (add lines 1a through 1c) (attach schedule—see instructions) (cash $ _____ noncash $ _____)	1d	
2	Program service revenue including government fees and contracts (from Part VII, line 93)	2	
3	Membership dues and assessments (see instructions)	3	
4	Interest on savings and temporary cash investments	4	
5	Dividends and interest from securities	5	
6a	Gross rents	6a	
b	Less: rental expenses	6b	
c	Net rental income or (loss) (subtract line 6b from line 6a)	6c	
7	Other investment income (describe ►)	7	

8a	Gross amount from sale of assets other than inventory	(A) Securities	(B) Other	
		8a		
b	Less: cost or other basis and sales expenses.	8b		
c	Gain or (loss) (attach schedule)	8c		
d	Net gain or (loss) (combine line 8c, columns (A) and (B))			8d

9	Special events and activities (attach schedule—see instructions):		
a	Gross revenue (not including $ _____ of contributions reported on line 1a)	9a	
b	Less: direct expenses other than fundraising expenses .	9b	
c	Net income or (loss) from special events (subtract line 9b from line 9a)	9c	
10a	Gross sales of inventory, less returns and allowances . .	10a	
b	Less: cost of goods sold	10b	
c	Gross profit or (loss) from sales of inventory (attach schedule) (subtract line 10b from line 10a) .	10c	
11	Other revenue (from Part VII, line 103)	11	
12	**Total revenue** (add lines 1d, 2, 3, 4, 5, 6c, 7, 8d, 9c, 10c, and 11)	12	

Expenses

13	Program services (from line 44, column (B)—see instructions)	13	
14	Management and general (from line 44, column (C)—see instructions)	14	
15	Fundraising (from line 44, column (D)—see instructions)	15	
16	Payments to affiliates (attach schedule—see instructions)	16	
17	**Total expenses** (add lines 16 and 44, column (A))	17	

Net Assets

18	Excess or (deficit) for the year (subtract line 17 from line 12)	18	
19	Net assets or fund balances at beginning of year (from line 74, column (A))	19	
20	Other changes in net assets or fund balances (attach explanation)	20	
21	Net assets or fund balances at end of year (combine lines 18, 19, and 20)	21	

For Paperwork Reduction Act Notice, see page 1 of the separate instructions.   Cat. No. 11282Y   Form **990** (1994)

Exhibit 2–18

Form **990-T**	**Exempt Organization Business Income Tax Return**	OMB No. 1545-0687
	(and proxy tax under section 6033(e))	
Department of the Treasury Internal Revenue Service	For calendar year 1994 or other tax year beginning _____ , 1994, and ending _____ , 19___ ▶ **See separate instructions.**	**1994**

A ☐ Check box if address changed		Name of organization	D Employer identification number (Employee's trust, see instructions for Block D)
B Exempt under section ☐ 501(X) or ☐ 408(e)	**Please Print or Type**	Number, street, and room or suite no. (If a P.O. box, see page 5 of instructions.)	E Unrelated business activity codes (see instructions for Block E)
C Book value of all assets at end of year		City or town, state, and ZIP code	

F Group exemption number (see instructions for Block F) ▶

G Check type of organization. ▶ ☐ 501 (C)Corporation ☐ 501(C) Trust ☐ Section 401(a) trust ☐ Section 408(a) trust

H Describe the organization's primary unrelated business activity. (See instructions for Block H)

I During the tax year, was the corporation a subsidiary in an affiliated group or a parent-subsidiary controlled group? ▶ ☐ Yes ☐ No

If "Yes," enter the name and identifying number of the parent corporation. (See instructions for Block I) ▶

Part I Unrelated Trade or Business Income

			(A) Income	(B) Expenses	(C) Net
1a	Gross receipts or sales _____				
b	Less returns and allowances _____ c Balance ▶	1c			
2	Cost of goods sold (Schedule A, line 7)	2			
3	Gross profit (subtract line 2 from line 1c)	3			
4a	Capital gain net income (attach Schedule D)	4a			
b	Net gain (loss) (Form 4797, Part II, line 20) (attach Form 4797)	4b			
c	Capital loss deduction for trusts	4c			
5	Income (loss) from partnerships (attach statement)	5			
6	Rent income (Schedule C)	6			
7	Unrelated debt-financed income (Schedule E)	7			
8	Interest, annuities, royalties, and rents from controlled organizations (Schedule F)	8			
9	Investment income of a section 501(c)(7), (9), or (17) organization (Schedule G)	9			
10	Exploited exempt activity income (Schedule I)	10			
11	Advertising income (Schedule J)	11			
12	Other income (see instructions – attach schedule)	12			
13	TOTAL (combine lines 3 through 12)	13			

Part II Deductions Not Taken Elsewhere (See instructions for limitations on deductions.)
(Except for contributions, deductions must be directly connected with the unrelated business income.)

14	Compensation of officers, directors, and trustees (Schedule K)	14	
15	Salaries and wages	15	
16	Repairs and maintenance	16	
17	Bad debts	17	
18	Interest (attach schedule)	18	
19	Taxes and licenses	19	
20	Charitable contributions (see instructions for limitation rules)	20	
21	Depreciation (attach Form 4562) 21		
22	Less depreciation claimed on Schedule A and elsewhere on return 22a	22b	
23	Depletion	23	
24	Contributions to deferred compensation plans	24	
25	Employee benefit programs	25	
26	Excess exempt expenses (Schedule I)	26	
27	Excess readership costs (Schedule J)	27	
28	Other deductions (attach schedule)	28	
29	TOTAL DEDUCTIONS (add lines 14 through 28)	29	
30	Unrelated business taxable income before net operating loss deduction (subtract line 29 from line 13)	30	
31	Net operating loss deduction	31	
32	Unrelated business taxable income before specific deduction (subtract line 31 from line 30)	32	
33	Specific deduction	33	
34	Unrelated business taxable income (subtract line 33 from line 32). If line 33 is greater than line 32, enter the smaller of zero or line 32	34	

423701 12-20-94 S430 **For Paperwork Reduction Act Notice, see page 1 of separate instructions.** Form **990-T** (1994)

Exhibit 2–19

Form 1040-ES
Department of the Treasury
Internal Revenue Service

1995 Payment Voucher **3**

OMB No. 1545-0087

Calendar year – Due Sept. 15, 1995

File only if you are making a payment of estimated tax. Return this voucher with check or money order payable to the **"Internal Revenue Service."** Please write your social security number and "1995 Form 1040-ES" on your check or money order. Please do not send cash. Enclose, but do not staple or attach, your payment with this voucher.

Amount of payment	Please type or print	Your first name and initial	Your last name	Your social security number
		If joint payment, complete for spouse		
		Spouse's first name and initial	Spouse's last name	Spouse's social security number
$ _ _ _ _ _ _ _ _ _ _ _ _		Address (number, street, and apt. no.)		
		City, state, and ZIP code. (If a foreign address, enter city, province or state, postal code, and country.)		

S430 For Paperwork Reduction Act Notice, see instructions on page 1.

- CUT HERE -

Form 1040-ES
Department of the Treasury
Internal Revenue Service

1995 Payment Voucher **2**

OMB No. 1545-0087

Calendar year – Due June 15, 1995

File only if you are making a payment of estimated tax. Return this voucher with check or money order payable to the **"Internal Revenue Service."** Please write your social security number and "1995 Form 1040-ES" on your check or money order. Please do not send cash. Enclose, but do not staple or attach, your payment with this voucher.

Amount of payment	Please type or print	Your first name and initial	Your last name	Your social security number
		If joint payment, complete for spouse		
		Spouse's first name and initial	Spouse's last name	Spouse's social security number
$ _ _ _ _ _ _ _ _ _ _ _ _		Address (number, street, and apt. no.)		
		City, state, and ZIP code. (If a foreign address, enter city, province or state, postal code, and country.)		

S430 For Paperwork Reduction Act Notice, see instructions on page 1.

- CUT HERE -

Form 1040-ES
Department of the Treasury
Internal Revenue Service

1995 Payment Voucher **1**

OMB No. 1545-0087

Calendar year – Due April 17, 1995

File only if you are making a payment of estimated tax. Return this voucher with check or money order payable to the **"Internal Revenue Service."** Please write your social security number and "1995 Form 1040-ES" on your check or money order. Please do not send cash. Enclose, but do not staple or attach, your payment with this voucher.

Amount of payment	Please type or print	Your first name and initial	Your last name	Your social security number
		If joint payment, complete for spouse		
		Spouse's first name and initial	Spouse's last name	Spouse's social security number
$ _ _ _ _ _ _ _ _ _ _ _ _		Address (number, street, and apt. no.)		
		City, state, and ZIP code. (If a foreign address, enter city, province or state, postal code, and country.)		

S430 For Paperwork Reduction Act Notice, see instructions on page 1.

- CUT HERE -

410411
12-18-94

46

Chapter 3

The Medical Liability for Your Church

The legal gloves are off! Churches are no longer treated with a special appreciation and respect when it comes to being sued. Hundreds of lawsuits are brought against churches every year—many of which could have been prevented.

Medical injuries are a common area of liability risk exposure. Whether mishaps occur on an outside trip or on the premises themselves, the church does have a certain amount of responsibility. Aside from purchasing an appropriate amount of medical injury liability insurance, what can a church reasonably do to protect itself?

Use a Medical Consent Form

When trips or events are involved, be especially certain every minor has a current and signed medical consent form on file prior to leaving church property. Medical consent forms should include emergency information, such as a name, address, and phone number, and various check-off boxes listing allergies or noteworthy medical problems. It should also include the date and a signature line for the parent/guardian.

Use a Consent & Release from Liability Form

This form should include a statement that acknowledges that the participant is aware of the mode of transportation, is cognizant of the dangers involved in the activity, and agrees to accept all risks of injury as a result of participation in this particular event.

Suggestion: To keep it simple and to ensure that the forms are current, combine both forms into one and then add them to a registration form. When the individual signs up for the event, he or she must also complete the release forms.

A Further Precaution: Many churches require a signed medical/liability release form for all adults participating in organized athletic events. If someone is injured in a church basketball league, who pays?

More Than an Ounce of Prevention

Although it is nearly impossible to absolve a church from all medically related risks, the church can take steps to demonstrate its awareness of the potential of negligence and the fact that it does not take its responsibility in this area lightly:

✔ At least one individual who is working with a group of minors should be certified in first aid and CPR (and be aware of any pertinent adverse medical histories). If no one is qualified to handle a particular injury, competent help should be sought. A church can be liable when an unqualified worker assists and complicates injuries.

✔ A basic first-aid kit (with splints, bandages, and compresses) should be accessible to a trained individual at all church events, with enough supplies to treat at least ten people. Three Band-Aids® and iodine aren't enough!

✔ All church vehicle drivers should have current licenses (public passenger or chauffeur licenses may be required to drive church vans and buses), have had their driving records checked, and be thoroughly familiar with the type of vehicles they are operating. If it could be proven that the church exercised "Negligent Selection" (legalese for "We don't care who drives the bus—just get somebody!"), you've got problems. This means that when unqualified or improperly licensed people are allowed to drive church-owned vehicles, the costs for all the medical injuries could be levied against the church. Why not lower that probability by selecting only those drivers who are qualified?

✔ In the event of an accident or injury, qualified church workers should be instructed to treat the injured person as a first priority and refrain from discussing with the injured person who is at fault or guilty. Although this may sound coldhearted, it is a good practice. Either the injured party's insurance carrier or the church's will no doubt get involved, and it isn't helpful when a church worker accepts guilt on behalf of the church simply to make the injured person feel better. Those kinds of statements can be used against the church later, even though the injured person does not want to sue the church. Unfortunately, insurance companies do their utmost to shift blame to others.

It is advisable that a minimum of $1 million in liability insurance be carried by the church to protect itself in the event of an accident or injury. Have the policy reviewed by your agent annually to be certain coverage is adequate and in force.

Exhibit 3–1
Parental Consent Forms

PARENTAL CONSENT FORM
Travel in Private Vehicles

I, _____ , approve of and authorize the
(Parent of Guardian)

transporting of my child, _____ , to _____
(Name of minor)   (Destination)

in a private vehicle. This event will take place on _____ between
(Date)

the hours of _____ and _____ .

_____   _____
Parent or Guardian   Date

REGISTRATION AND MEDICAL CONSENT FORM

Name: _____ Phone: _____
Address: _____ City and State: _____ Zip: _____
Dates of Activity: _____ Birthdate: _____ Sex: _____

EMERGENCY NOTIFICATION   ALTERNATE CONTACT
Name: _____   Name: _____
Home Phone: _____   Home Phone: _____
Work Phone: _____   Work Phone: _____

HEALTH HISTORY

ALLERGIES   ❏ Diabetes   ❏ Emotional Handicap
❏ Drugs   ❏ Cardiac   ❏ Mental Handicap
❏ Asthma   ❏ Chronic Asthma   ❏ Seizure Disorder
❏ Hay Fever   ❏ Nervous Disorder   ❏ Other
❏ Insect Stings   ❏ Epilepsy   Date of last
❏ Other   ❏ Physical Handicap   Tetanus Shot _____

If you have checked any of the above, please give details_____
Activity Restriction:_____
This health history is correct, so far as I know. I hereby give my permission to the physician, nurse, or dentist selected
by the _____ (church) to secure medical and dental aid as required for illness or injury under a
physician's orders, including transportation to and from the necessary facilities. *(Use back of form for any explanations.)*

_____Signature _____Date
(Parent or guardian, if registrant is minor or dependent)

CONSENT AND RELEASE FROM LIABILITY

I, _____ , hereby acknowledge that it is my desire (for my child) to participate in
church-sponsored activities at _____ (church), including activities on and/or away from the
church premises as well as transportation to and from such activities.

I AM (MY CHILD IS) VOLUNTARILY PARTICIPATING IN THESE ACTIVITIES, INCLUDING TRANSPORTATION TO AND FROM
SUCH ACTIVITIES, WITH KNOWLEDGE OF THE DANGERS INVOLVED AND HEREBY AGREE TO ACCEPT ANY AND ALL RISKS
OF INJURY AS A RESULT OF SUCH PARTICIPATION AND TRANSPORTATION.

As lawful consideration for permitting me (my child) to participate in such activities, including the transportation to and from such
activities, I hereby release and discharge _____ (church), its officers, employees, agents and members
of the Board of Trustees from all actions, claims or demands I and my heirs, distributees, guardians, legal representatives or
assigns now have or may hereafter have for any injury or damages resulting from the negligence or other acts, howsoever caused,
by such church, officers, employees, agents and Board of Trustees, before or during my participation in such church-sponsored
activities on and/or away from the church premises, including transportation to and from such activities.

I HAVE CAREFULLY READ THIS AGREEMENT AND FULLY UNDERSTAND ITS CONTENTS. I AM AWARE THAT THIS IS A
RELEASE OF LIABILITY AND AN ASSUMPTION OF RISKS AND SIGN IT OF MY OWN FREE WILL.

This Consent and Release From Liability shall remain effective until revoked in writing and delivered to any officer, employee or
agent of _____ (church).

Executed this _____ day of _____ , 19 ____ , at _____ .

_____
Signature

49

Chapter 4

The Potential for Child Abuse and Child Abuse Lawsuits

C hild sexual abuse within the setting of the local church is surfacing as the most common grounds for litigation against churches today. What makes this a most tragic crime is the assumption that a young person would and should be safe from this type of offense within the confines of a church. Although child sexual abuse regardless of race, age, and social background, it has a tendency to be more objectionable when it happens at a church or church-sponsored event. Such lawsuits typically claim negligent hiring, supervision, or the retention of a person who is accused of child molestation.

Why a Church Needs to Protect Itself

Al Davidson, vice president of claims for Brotherhood Mutual Insurance Company, says, "Churches are refusing to do anything about [child sexual abuse]." He asserts that churches "won't suspect or confront anyone." This particular insurance company now has more than fifty claims pending concerning sexually deviant behavior, and the claims keep coming in at the rate of one per month. According to Davidson, the company had no claims in dispute ten years ago.

Sexual abuse *can* happen in your church—don't kid yourself. The primary problem is that most churches are anxious to accept volunteers in the youth and children's programs, thankfully and nonjudgmentally. Good attendance and a willing attitude are thought to be signs of "faithfulness" and a "servant's heart." However, as noble as these qualities may appear, they are also the characteristics of a molester who is seeking victims.

That it may never happen doesn't mean it won't! It takes only one incident that reaches the attention of the public to destroy a church's reputation in the community. There is also the emotional trauma to the victim and to the victim's family, and the possible large financial settlement costs facing the church.

But a church *can* protect itself in this area. Although it is impossible to eliminate any and all chances of abuse, steps can be taken to lessen the risk and reduce the liability.

How a Church Can Protect Itself

In the process of litigating cases of this nature, the question most likely to be asked by the victim's lawyer is, "What steps did your church take to prevent this type of act from occurring?" That is a valid question, and one church leaders should be asking themselves.

A four-step plan should be followed:

1. Selecting volunteers and staff
2. Supervising volunteers and staff
3. Reporting obligations
4. Dealing with allegations[5]

Selection

It is important to have a screening process for all present and prospective workers. Failure to take this aspect of the plan seriously can easily open the church to charges of negligence. Although state laws vary as to the content of a specific form, a sample form has been provided. (See Exhibit 4–1.) It is also a good idea to go over the completed form with the worker to confirm orally what was stated in writing.

Supervision

Always have two adults present (preferably above the age of twenty-one) during all church activities. This rule reduces both the risk of molestation as well as the risk of false accusations. In those cases where an adult has a legitimate reason to be alone with a young person, parental or guardian consent should be sought.

It is also wise to discuss the laws and criminal sanctions with all the youth workers. Impress upon them the seriousness of this issue and the personal consequences to them as individuals.

5. These steps are adapted from Hammar, Klipowicz, and Cobble, "Reducing the Risk of Child Sexual Abuse in Your Church," *Church Law & Tax Report* (1993).

Reporting

Every state has mandatory reporting rules. They include what constitutes child abuse, who is legally responsible to report abuse, and how long after being made aware of the abuse a person is required to make a report (24 or 48 hours; oral or written).

Responding to Charges

The wrong response to an allegation, whether it is true or false, can complicate and possibly aggravate the situation. This could translate into more pain for the victims and liability for the church.

✔ Take all allegations seriously.

✔ Situations are to be handled with privacy and respect.

✔ Contact your insurance carrier immediately.

✔ Cooperate fully with civil authorities.

✔ Show genuine concern and care for the victims.

There is much more that can be learned about this vital subject. Books, tapes, workshops, and consultants are available through various sources. Above all, this is one of those times when doing nothing only deepens the potential for harm to potential victims and for liability for the church.

Additional Resources

Policies and Procedures Manual, Brotherhood Mutual Insurance Company, Indianapolis, Indiana.

Books and tapes are available through Christian Ministry Resources, P.O. Box 1098, Matthews, NC 28106.

Exhibit 4–1
Youth Worker Application

This application is an effort on the part of our church to determine the suitability and giftedness of those who work with our youth. Please do not think that we are being overly careful or trying to delve into your private life. The information on this form will be kept in strict confidence. The information you give to us will assist the church in the event that any false accusations are brought against you.

We appreciate your willingness to work in this vital ministry area and the time you take to complete this form. Thank you.

Date: _____

Name: _____
　　　　　　　Last　　　　　　　　　First　　　　　　　　Middle

Address: _____

City: _____ State: _____ Zip: _____

Home Phone (　　) _____ Work Phone (　　) _____

Please attach a copy of your current driver's license.

List past experience working with youth. This should include both church and non-church involvement. (Use a separate page if necessary.)

List the people we may contact as references from each of your past ministry situations.

Which area of youth work ministry would you prefer?

What is the minimum length of time and weekly hours you could commit to?

What is your preferred start date?

Have you ever been convicted of a crime? Yes _____ No _____

If yes, please explain. What is your legal status as of this date? (Use a separate page if necessary.)

Were you ever a victim of molestation or sexual abuse as a minor? (You may refuse to answer this question if you prefer, or you may discuss the answer with the senior pastor. Your discussion will be kept confidential. Leaving the answer blank will not disqualify you automatically.)

Please supply us with at least two references. These should not be family members.

Name _____   Name _____

Address _____   Address _____

_____   _____

Phone _____   Phone _____

The information contained in this application is accurate to the best of my knowledge. I agree that, if I am accepted to work with the youth of the church, I will abide by the bylaws of the church and conform to all the teachings regarding biblical moral conduct.

I also give the church permission to contact those references I have listed and any former organizations I have worked for to verify the facts contained in this application.

Furthermore, I waive the right to inspect any information provided about me from those I have identified and those you contact listed in this application.

I have read all the information contained on this form, and I understand that it is legally binding.

Signature of Applicant: _____

Date: _____

Witness: _____

Date: _____

NOTE: This form is for illustrative purposes only. Please contact an attorney in your state to determine the correct wording and format of an application to use in the screening of youth workers.

Section 2
Church Finances

Chapter 5

Introduction to Church Finances

The headline in the *Los Angeles Times* read "Popular Preacher Finds Himself Beset by Probes of Fraud." A few years earlier, an article in the *Wall Street Journal* was entitled "Church Bonds Plunge into Default." "Church Official Gets Five Years in Tax Scheme" was reported in another large-city newspaper.

Today's church often makes headlines for the wrong reasons. Public details of financial misdeeds by pastors and church boards are becoming all too common. "Forgive us our debts" has taken on a new sense of urgency in recent years. References to "Chapter XI" are being heard in board meetings more frequently. Unfortunately, the context has nothing to do with a chapter reference in the Bible.[6]

The term *stewardship* has come to represent financial obligation on the part of the donor. Usually the intent of the word is directed toward a congregation, reminding them of their responsibility as it relates to their giving. As the dictionary defines the term, however, a *steward* is "one who manages another's property or financial affairs." It can be illustrated by the role a bank plays. A bank is responsible for other people's money and is expected to provide protection as well as a reasonable return on the investment. In the context of the local church, its pastor and leaders also have a duty to properly manage the funds placed in their care.

As is the case with any other business organization, the complexity of a church's financial procedures is generally directly related to its size. A system that would be adequate for a church with a membership of fifty or sixty will probably not be adequate for one with a membership of five or six hundred. Although the complexity changes with size, the basic objectives of any accounting system remain basically the same.

---

6. Chapter XI is a part of the Federal Bankruptcy Code and provides a means whereby a financially distressed business may restructure its finances and continue its operation for a period of time.

Objectives of a Church Accounting System

The primary objectives of a church accounting system are generally as follows.

1. The Proper Protection of Cash and Other Assets

Protection of assets is a basic objective of all accounting systems. Since funds contributed to a church no longer belong to the individual but to the Lord, even greater care should be exercised than what a businessman would exercise in his business. The systems and procedures outlined in this book are designed to help insure the safe handling of funds.

2. Use of Funds for the Purpose for Which They Were Contributed

If the church accepts gifts designated for a particular purpose that falls outside the church budget, the donors must be assured that the funds will be used in accordance with their wishes. (This issue will be covered more fully in chapter 9.)

An essential element of a church accounting system is that it provides an accurate record of individual giving. Since contributions to a church are permitted as an itemized deduction for federal and state income tax purposes, church officers may be called upon to verify contributions that have been claimed as a deduction by members or friends of the church. The availability of accurate information to provide appropriate substantiation to government agencies is therefore important.

Also, an accurate historical record of income and expenses is necessary to properly review past periods and make comparisons with current periods. A comparison of cash income and expense summaries for past periods can be helpful in budget preparation and future planning. This information may also provide insight as to God's direction in a particular area, such as a new building program.

Meeting the Objectives

This chapter is intended to provide guidance to leaders of local churches as they deal with the financial aspects of church administration. The content of the material presented is stated in such a manner as to provide sufficient detail so that even those with little or no accounting experience will find it useful. The suggested procedures and forms have been designed so that only a minimum of accounting knowledge is required.[7]

7. Acknowledgment to Paul Stolz, *Manual of Church Financial Procedures* (n.p., 1969).

Because of the differences in size and organizational structure of churches, a variety of different financial and accounting methods are being used by churches today. The objectives of a good accounting system, however, can usually be achieved without the need to change the church's organizational structure. The approach of this chapter is to speak in general terms so that the objectives can be met within the framework of the existing organizational structure.

The Right Standards

In recent years, concerns have been raised over the ethics and legality of the methods some churches use in the handling of funds. Some of these center on the following areas:

- The improper use of designated gifts
- Property tax exemptions when facilities are used for other than church activities
- The selling of unregistered securities
- Diversion of church donations to private use
- Unreasonable benefits or prerequisites being taken by members of the clergy
- The operation of profit-making business activities
- Questionable business activities
- Unfair treatment of employees

Several years ago, a group of concerned financial officers from both church and parachurch organizations had the foresight to recognize the coming danger. Sloppy bookkeeping, unethical fund-raising techniques, and the misappropriation of donated monies raised many questions in their minds. In 1979, the Evangelical Council for Financial Accountability (ECFA) was formed for the purpose of establishing basic standards of financial accountability for Christian organizations. To date, the ECFA has been quite effective in its role of promoting professional standards of financial responsibility.

The Right Perspective

Those individuals who must deal with the financial aspects of managing a church have a duty both to their congregations and to the Lord. The responsibility is one of a fiduciary—that is, one who is charged with a confidence or trust as it relates to the management of someone else's money. In fact, the biblical exhortation is clear: "We have regard for what is honorable, not only in the sight of the Lord, but also in the sight of men" (2 Corinthians 8:21).

The Right People

It is extremely important, therefore, that those individuals who are charged with the oversight of the financial resources of a church be of the highest caliber. You would think that a policy such as this would be a foregone conclusion, especially in a church. Unfortunately, that isn't always the case. Repeatedly, situations have come up where financial officers were selected simply because they were "good with money." Perhaps the man is a successful businessman, has the largest farm in the community, or, worst of all, is the biggest contributor. If these are the only prerequisites to being the church financial officer, the church is flirting with potential problems. Who *should* serve then? Those men and women who have demonstrated their faithfulness to previously assigned tasks and who evidence the biblical character qualities outlined later in this chapter.

To develop and carry out a good accounting system, it is helpful for certain individuals and committees to be involved. The titles given to these committees and positions may vary from church to church; however, the titles are not that important. The key is the role they fill in carrying out this vital function.

There may be an overlap between the duties of these committees even to the extent that one committee may perform the function of all groups listed. This would be controlled to some extent by the size of the church. It is absolutely essential, however, that the individual offices listed below be maintained as separate offices. To combine the positions of treasurer and financial secretary, for example, is to destroy the basic concept of internal control necessary for a good accounting system. (Internal control will be explained more fully later in this chapter.) Therefore, these positions should be kept separate even in the smallest church.

Here is a list of the officers and committees:

- *Treasurer*: This officer is entrusted with the receipt, care, and disbursement of funds.
- *Financial Secretary*: This is an individual who receives the church offering envelopes, special offering envelopes, receipts and other evidences of money received, and a summary of receipts from money counters for posting to individual members' records.
- *Finance Committee*: A committee usually consisting of three to five members, including the treasurer and financial secretary, it has the responsibility for overseeing the fiscal affairs of the church.
- *Budget Committee*: An ad hoc, or temporary, committee, this group may be composed of the members of the finance committee, or it may be expanded to include others. This committee is responsible for preparation of the annual church budget. In a larger church, that would include assembling the budget requests of various boards or departments for inclusion into an overall church budget plan.
- *Counting Committee*: For a larger church, it might be advisable to form a counting committee. This committee may be composed of some of the members of the finance committee and may also include others. It is their responsibility to receive, count, and deposit church funds.

✔ *Audit Committee*: In a very large church an audit committee would be useful. It should be composed of at least three members. These people may be from the finance committee, be trustees of the church, or be separately appointed or elected. It is the duty of this committee to oversee the audit of the financial records of the church annually or as instructed by the church. If the church is too small for an audit committee, then the ruling board could appoint one or two people who are not on any of the financial groups to review the records.

The financial officers of the church don't necessarily need to be accountants or CPAs. The most practical and effective minimum standard for a financial steward (that is, a money counter, bookkeeper, financial secretary, or treasurer) should be that of being a deacon or wife of a deacon. The qualifications are outlined clearly for us in 1 Timothy 3:8–13 and Titus 1:6–9. Ideally, you would want your highest offices filled by people qualified as—to use New Testament terminology—elders, deacons, or wives of deacons. Starting with the requirements of an elder, or overseer, and moving on through those of a deacon, we find a common thread, a continuous theme—trustworthiness:

✔ *Above reproach*—a good reputation in and outside the church (1 Timothy 3:2, 7)

✔ *Temperate*—does things in moderation (1 Timothy 3:2)

✔ *Prudent*—is shrewd (in a good sense), cautious, and thrifty (1 Timothy 3:2)

✔ *Respectable*—one who is deserving of high regard (1 Timothy 3:2)

✔ *Free from the love of money*—the pursuit of money does not become a preoccupation (1 Timothy 3:3)

✔ *Manages his own household well*—refers to both people and resources (1 Timothy 3:4, 12)

Titus 1:7 sums it up: "The overseer must be above reproach as God's steward." A person can't help but use the word *integrity* in describing this faithful servant. Integrity has been defined as "doing what you're supposed to do when no one is looking." The risk factor in selecting those individuals who are charged with the handling of funds can be greatly reduced when they are chosen on the basis of their character traits first instead of by their secular abilities.

The point is simple: If a person evidences biblical maturity, the likelihood of securing the services of an honest individual are greatly enhanced. If, on the other hand, officers are chosen primarily on the basis of professional prowess, the potential for future problems is increased.

Good people are an essential ingredient to the success of good policies.

Internal Control

A pastor once told me, "I just don't understand all that financial stuff, so I have one of my deacons take care of it!" If your church is small, perhaps your money handling and bookkeeping procedures are quite simple and you feel comfortable with a volunteer handling the load. And that's fine—to a point. However, in order for a medium- to large-size church to function properly today—with the heightened demands for security, the need to protect the church's tax exemption, and the obligation to act responsibly with God's money—some formal system and procedures are a must.

Although it may sound rather technical, the major purposes of sound financial policies and procedures are as follows:

1. To monitor the performance of those charged with the management of funds
2. To provide clear and accurate information to donors and church leadership
3. To protect the assets of the organization

Internal control, as defined in this chapter, is "the coordination of methods and measures adopted by an organization to check the accuracy and validity of data and to safeguard assets."[8]

When a proper system of internal control is in place, more than one person will be involved in almost all transactions, especially those relating to cash. This provides a natural check of one against the other, which should not be viewed as distrust but merely a form of protection and accountability. It is essential that a church maintain good internal control in not just cash procedures but in all the other accounting areas as well.

Checkpoints

Aside from the obvious requirement to ensure the public that the ministry is not being defrauded, the people who actually handle funds need to be protected from outside charges of wrongdoing. To do this, there should be established cash flow "checkpoints," that is, an internal system of accountability.

Within a church context, there is a general path or route funds travel as they move from the collection plate (receipts) to the process of paying the bills (disbursements). In most smaller churches, one person (usually the bookkeeper or treasurer) oversees all these functions. No matter how small the congregation may be, however, this area should be given a closer look. If necessary, a flow chart of the path of money through the church can help to identify potential improvements or weaknesses in the system.

The Collection

The handling of cash itself does not result in a permanent, written record until the funds are deposited into the bank. Most other components of the church accounting

8. Jerry Rosenberg, *Dictionary of Business and Management* (New York: John Wiler, 1978), 231.

system will produce written records as natural by-products. For example, a cash disbursement in the form of a check will produce a canceled check and a bank statement that can be reviewed at a later date. Therefore, the establishment of a good procedure for the handling of cash may be more important than any other area.

The first checkpoint is actually made up of two functions: receiving the collection, and counting the money. For the protection of the ushers who receive the money, a certain degree of caution must be exercised, particularly if the offerings are large or the location of the church presents a high degree of risk from theft. If the ushers must carry the plates outside the auditorium itself, they should proceed in groups of no less than two but not all together as a single group. At no time should a single person be alone with one or more of the collection plates until such time as the funds are physically deposited in a secure place. This will help ensure maximum security of the money and protection for the ushers and will indicate to everyone the importance you place on the proper handling of the Lord's money.

Next, the money should be counted as soon after the collection is taken as practical. This should be done in a secure location, away from public view.

To protect the counters from outside comments or unnecessary problems, it is often a good idea to have these individuals serve on a rotating basis. This helps to protect the confidentiality of members' financial affairs and reduce knowledge of giving patterns.

Another reason for alternating counters is the need to prevent the same people from missing worship services every Sunday. A policy of rotation helps prevent this potential tragedy.

Offering envelopes should be opened individually and checked to determine if the amount on the outside is the same as the amount of money contained within the envelope. Or, if no amount is indicated on the envelope, the proper amount can be filled in. If the contributions are broken down into several funds, envelopes should be used with space provided on the front to enter the amount applicable to each fund. (See Exhibit 5–2.)

After the counting is completed, a summary report should be prepared for accounting purposes. A preprinted form, such as illustrated in Exhibit 5–1, can be especially helpful for this purpose.

Many times an envelope is received without any designation on it or without the donor's wishes being clearly indicated. The finance committee should establish a policy as to how to distribute such gifts. This policy should be approved by the church so that the individuals making contributions will be aware of it.

After the cash has been counted and reconciled, the "flow of funds" is continued to the actual depositing of the money. In some churches this function is performed solely by the treasurer. It is preferable, however, to have the counting committee prepare the actual deposit slip. The treasurer can still deposit the money even if the counting committee prepares the deposit slip.

Again, this procedure needs to be kept simple but secure. Try not to store funds on church premises overnight unless you have a good, fireproof safe. A floor safe is preferable because it cannot be carted away, and it is essential that the combination be known only by two or three individuals. Police officers tell me that churches are "easy pickins" for even amateur burglars. Security is often inadequate, and money is usually kept locked in desk drawers or file cabinets.

Although most churches have a safe with a combination lock available for temporary storage of cash, if no safe is available, the money could be counted during or immediately following the service and deposited the same day. Another good procedure is to put all the money, uncounted, in a bag and deposit it in the bank night deposit slot during the service. On Monday morning a counting team can go to the bank and count it. This avoids the need to store large sums of money on the church premises overnight or to reveal the combination of the church safe to a number of individuals.

Each time a different person is selected to a position that allows him or her to know the combination of the safe, the combination should be changed. If this procedure is not followed, in time there will be many people, with no accountability, who know the combination.

Some churches also carry insurance against theft of funds. Many times, however, these policies state that the insurance does not apply until the offering has been counted. Insurance policies should be examined for these provisions and every effort made to minimize the time interval between receiving an offering and counting it.

If money is deposited in a locked night bank depository, two men should accompany the funds to the bank; however, they should not travel together in the same car. Why? Once more, accountability and safety is the goal. (Detectives with the Los Angeles Police Department have suggested that churches use the two-car procedure.)

Since the morning services usually account for the largest offering, another alternative is to take Sunday morning's offerings to the bank immediately. Then the Sunday evening offering (which is generally much smaller) could either be deposited that night or stored in a safe location until Monday. The chance of theft is greater after dark, so the key here is to get the largest portion of the cash to the bank as soon as possible.

Disbursements—Check and Double-Check

Now that the money is safely tucked away in the bank, we move on to the next "checkpoint"—disbursements. Ideally, this area of internal control encompasses three procedures:

66

1. The same person who approves purchases should not prepare the checks for payment.
2. The individual who prepares the checks ideally should not be in a position to sign them.
3. The check signer should not complete the circle by also approving the invoices for payment.

The customary "trail" looks something like this:

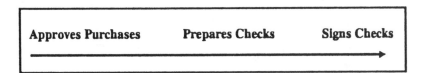

Good internal control would require a break in the direct line:

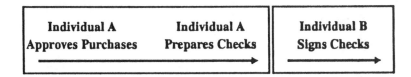

Different individuals can perform each step. The minimum standard would be to place a checkpoint between the functions of preparing and signing checks.

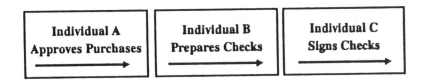

In many small churches, all these procedures may be performed by the same individual. Nevertheless, it is still preferable to have one of the functions handled by a second person.

A final checkpoint is to place a limit on the amount any one individual may draw in the form of a check (e.g., $250, $500). This amount should be determined at your ruling board's discretion and be based on the size and number of checks involved. For maximum protection, another means of limiting exposure in this area is to imprint your checks with "two signatures required for checks over $XXX," $XXX standing for a stipulated amount.

Recording Gifts

Most of the church's income is received through collection plates, and usually more than one person handles the funds. Since all money counters are human (robots haven't taken over this job—yet!), mistakes and temptations will be ever present. If the qualifications for financial stewards are set high enough, however, integrity and honesty will be an inherent part of the job description for this position.

The counting and depositing of funds was discussed previously. At this point, however, I'd like to move to another important element of church internal control: the record of individual giving.

The Envelope, Please!

Most churches use some form of preprinted envelope for offering purposes, though there are still some churches that resist such a system. An envelope system is essential both to developing a good internal cash control system and to contributing to sound accounting procedures. An envelope system produces an individual giving record for both the donor and the church.

In the business world, a record of financial transactions is almost always accompanied by an internal record, along with a receipt for the customer. The contributors to the church financial program likewise should receive some sort of verification of their gifts.

The most common envelope system consists of fifty-two numbered envelopes to correspond with each week of the year. These envelopes may also bear a number previously assigned to the donor and dates for each Sunday of the year. A system using assigned donor numbers serves to protect the privacy of the donor and facilitates the proper posting of contributions to the church records.

Many envelope companies also provide special offering envelopes for Easter, Thanksgiving, and Christmas. Envelopes featuring the church's logo or a picture of the church, Bible verses, or the church's motto may be easily obtained from your local church supply store or denominational headquarters.

Advantages of the Envelope System

In addition to the businesslike way of managing contributions, an envelope system also encourages systematic giving by providing an envelope for each week. The empty envelope is a reminder of the individual's responsibility toward systematic giving.

A complete envelope system will also provide givers with a periodic (quarterly) record of their gifts. The least the church should provide is a record of total contributions at the end of the year. If the donor notes a discrepancy between the summary and his own records, this difference should be called to the attention of the appointed financial officer, thus another cross-check.

Another added advantage of the envelope system is the fact that proper receipts and records are available for the donor to substantiate his claim for income tax deductions. Although the Internal Revenue Service used to allow canceled checks as proof of donations, they now require a statement from the church records as substantiation for gifts of cash and checks made out for more than $250. (See "Receipting Requirements" in chapter 2.)

Unfortunately, many people tend to give only when they are moved emotionally to do so. Don't misunderstand me—the Bible is clear on the fact that we are to give with some emotional attachment. Second Corinthians 9:7 tells us, "Each one must do just as he has purposed in his heart, not grudgingly or under compulsion, for God loves a cheerful giver." This verse teaches that giving is to be both purposeful (with forethought) and cheerful. There is certainly room for both emotion and budgeting in giving. The point is, the use of envelopes presupposes some prior thought and preparation for stewardship participation. It also promotes regularity in giving and sets a good example for children.

A final advantage is that all gifts in an envelope appear alike when they are given. Whether it be a large donation or the "widow's mite," it all looks the same. It's the givers' hearts that are different!

Keeping the Books

Though this chapter is designed to keep financial procedures simple, the following discussion may get a little complicated for the untrained person. Therefore, I'll attempt to stay with the basics.

Cash Receipts Journal

Assuming that cash has been properly counted and deposited, a record of the activity should be noted in a cash receipts journal. (See Exhibit 5–3.) By definition, a journal is a chronological record of original entry; it is the "front door" of a formal accounting system. Perhaps you've heard the term *ledger* used at one time or another. A ledger is a record of final entry—no more entries are put into the bookkeeping system after the ledger entry (more about that later).

The cash receipts journal should be maintained by the treasurer or another appropriate person, and the format may vary considerably from church to church. What is important is that the journal be designed to meet the specific needs and situation of the church where it is being used. The point is that you need to have one.

The format of the receipts journal depends on the kind of budget used by the church. Generally, there are two basic types: the traditional "fund" budget and the unified budget. The *fund budget* is one where monies are collected and placed in various designated funds or accounts to be disbursed for specific purposes—funds for missions, building projects, debt retirement, or any number of special areas of interest. (A general fund is usually one of those funds as well.) The *unified budget*, on the other hand, receives all income into one fund. Then all expenses are paid out of that one fund. Even with the unified budget format, however, it is not uncommon to have a separate building fund, because those gifts are often held in reserve for future building-related purposes.

Both budgeting methods require an understanding of the implications and the philosophy behind them, so full governing board approval should be obtained before switching from one to the other. A church with a unified budget will require a very simple cash receipts journal since practically no separation of receipts is necessary. In this situation, there will be one column for the cash deposited and another column for the offerings received. It would also be advisable to have a miscellaneous column to be used for unusual items not a part of the regular budget.

The cash receipts journal shown in Exhibit 5–3 is an example of what would be used by a church that is *not* on a unified budget. The column headings should be titled to match the budget categories of the individual church for which it is to be used. Essentially, it should contain one column for the total cash deposited and separate columns for each of the funds maintained by the church. Again, a miscellaneous column is included for special gifts and offerings not included in the regular, established funds.

The Procedure for Maintaining the Journal

1. The treasurer receives the duplicate of the bank deposit slip, plus one copy of the summary of receipts (Exhibit 5–1) from the counting committee.
2. From this slip he completes the "journalizing," that is, the entering of the cash received into the journal. This should be done by entering the total cash deposited in the debit "cash deposited" column and the details in those columns where they belong. The loose offering normally would be credited to the general fund unless there is some other policy established for distributing it. At the end of the month the columns are added to provide the totals for the receipts in each of the funds and the total cash deposited. After these totals have been determined, the sums should be cross-checked by adding up all the credits to make certain they are equal to the debit total in the "cash deposited" column.

Paying the Bills

To this point, we have dealt with the different aspects of the receiving and handling of funds. To be consistent with our goal of keeping the "mysteries" of accounting simple, I will continue to offer suggestions that lend themselves to the smaller church. A brief discussion of a more complex accounting method—double entry bookkeeping—will be dealt with later.

Continuing with our policy of maintaining good internal control, as far as possible all disbursements should be made by check. If a petty cash fund is used, it should be reimbursed at least monthly by issuing a check for the exact amount of the expenditures made from it. Receipts and other supporting data should be submitted to the treasurer at the time of reimbursing petty cash in the same manner as would be provided for paying any other bill.

The purpose of having cash on hand (hopefully in a locked box) is to pay for those expenses that are small and immediate. This avoids the time and expense required to process a check for inconsequential items.

The matter of cosigning checks has been discussed previously. Normally, only one signature is required on a check for smaller amounts. The cosigner for larger checks should be the treasurer or some other responsible person who is in an accountable position in the financial stream of the organization. An additional signatory allows checks to be written if the treasurer is out of town or is otherwise unavailable.

In some churches, two signatures are required on each and every check, no matter what the amount may be. While this provides a strong checkpoint of accountability, it can be cumbersome for the treasurer, who is usually a layperson and not always readily available.

The middle ground in this area would be to have a policy stating that all checks in excess of a particular amount be countersigned. The checks should be made out completely by the treasurer and signed by him prior to being submitted to the second party for the additional signature. Under no circumstances should blank checks be presigned.

Check Registers

Many forms of check registers (disbursement journals) are readily available and can be adapted to the needs of the local church. Deposits should be entered in the check register as well as in the cash receipts journal if you wish to maintain a running cash balance of the total in the bank account. Checks written for the payment of bills are entered in the columns provided and distributed to the column headed with the proper expenditure group. Column headings are normally used to separate items into groupings, such as those illustrated below. The correct account number (or account name) is assigned to each item as it is distributed. If the check register has additional columns available, a column may be assigned to an individual account for those accounts used most frequently. The miscellaneous column is used for items that do not occur frequently enough to warrant a column of their own. The items in each column should be summarized at the bottom, except for those columns assigned to a single account.

Account numbers should be designated to each specific account, as it will greatly facilitate the distribution of expenses in the check register. To simplify identification, these account numbers are usually assigned in different "hundred" or "thousand" groups to correspond to the different types of accounts:

General Fund

Physical Plant

401	Heat
402	Utilities
403	Salaries

General Fund

4010—1000	Heat—Church
4010—2000	Heat—School
4020—1000	Utilities—Church
4020—2000	Utilities—School

(See the sample chart of accounts in Exhibit 5–4 for more details.)

Whether it be a simple bookkeeping system or one using computers with a large volume of checks, a voucher-type check is highly recommended. This type of check has a voucher attached to it upon which the purpose of the payment is explained. A duplicate of each check can then be retained in the church's accounting files.

It is important that each column in the check register be completely filled in. If the check register you are using has the lines preprinted with check numbers, these numbers should not be ignored. The actual check number of each item should also be entered. At the end of the month, the columns in the check register should be totaled and a new page started for recording checks written in the following month. Any space remaining on the page can be used for recapping and other special comments.

Chart of Accounts

Every church bookkeeping system, no matter what the size, needs to have a proper chart of accounts. A chart of accounts is a formal listing of all the different accounts used by the church. Usually, the chart of accounts has numbers assigned to each account to help identify accounts and to more readily locate the account in the general ledger. Every account in the general ledger is listed in the chart of accounts—all assets, liabilities, income, and expenses. The chart of accounts is an index to facilitate bookkeeping.

It is impossible to provide a suggested chart of accounts that would be fully applicable in every situation. A small church does not need as elaborate a breakdown as is needed in a large church, and a church operating on a unified budget will have a chart of accounts that differs considerably from a church using a number of separate funds.

It does not matter whether the chart of accounts is large or small; the use of the account numbers is still important. Using an account number to identify an account will save a considerable amount of time and provide records that are neater and easier to follow.

The suggested chart of accounts provided in Exhibit 5–4 is for illustration purposes only and is based on a church with the following four funds:

General Fund

Missions Fund

Building Fund

Special Funds

The last of these, special funds, is really not one fund but many funds created for special purposes and closed out when that purpose is accomplished. For example, taking a special offering for camp scholarships would create a special fund that will be eliminated as soon as the funds are disbursed as designated by the purpose of this offering.

The needs of a local church must be considered in setting up a chart of accounts. The method of breaking down general fund disbursements may be done in a number of ways. Just try to use a method that provides the most information with the least amount of detail.

The numbering system presented here is not "chiseled in stone," nor is it the last word in charts of accounts. It is only a guide. However, it is best to use a numbering system that groups the accounts according to logical divisions. A numbering system that allows for four digits instead of two or three allows for future growth or the addition of subaccounts without having to continually be changing the basic numbering system. (See Exhibit 5–4.)

Double Entry System

To this point we have been discussing journals relating to "single entry systems." In a single entry system, the journal becomes the place of original entry as well as the summarization of accounts. When a financial report is prepared, the treasurer must go through the journals for the months involved and add up the totals to arrive at the figures to be inserted in the report. This procedure is adequate for smaller churches and is usually used where personnel are not available who have accounting or double entry bookkeeping experience.

Where experienced people are available, or in larger church situations, a double entry system is highly desirable. In a double entry system, in addition to the journals that have already been discussed, a general journal is set up that is used for the purpose of opening entries, adjusting entries, and closing entries. Anyone familiar with double entry bookkeeping is familiar with a general journal. Each month the summary totals are posted from the journals to a general ledger. A general ledger contains a page for each account in the chart of accounts. Each of these pages contains a debit, credit, and balance column. Each month the debits and credits from the general journal, cash receipts journal, and disbursements journal (check register) are posted to the general ledger. After completion of the posting, an adding machine tape is run on the balances to make sure the general ledger is in balance (or a computer bookkeeping program is used).

The advantage of maintaining a general ledger is that all the information is automatically summarized on a regular basis. This facilitates the preparation of periodic financial reports and eliminates errors that may otherwise be made in accumulating figures. Although it is not essential to have a double entry system in order to maintain good accounting records for a church, it is highly desirable to do so whenever the opportunity is available.

The simplest form of double entry system includes the cash account as the only asset account. Other accounts are income or receipts and disbursements as have already been designated in the chart of accounts. Under this simplified form, liability accounts for mortgages are not established. Liability accounts would be established, however, for payroll taxes and other temporary liabilities that are automatically liquidated in the following month. Operating expenses are usually not accrued but are recorded as paid on a "cash" basis.

It is also possible to establish a general ledger that would include asset accounts for buildings, land, equipment, and any other asset held by the church. Liability accounts would be established for mortgages and other obligations.

Just a word of sympathy for those who have just read this section on double entry systems and are saying, "This is too complicated for me!" I was told years ago that a wise man realizes when he is getting in over his head and knows where to go to get help. Please don't reject a double entry system just because you don't understand it. Get some professional assistance, and you'll see how helpful this system can be. The choice of the proper system for a particular church depends on the size of the church, the availability of qualified personnel, the desires of the church organization regarding financial reporting, and other local factors.

Other Considerations

Financial Reports

Financial reporting is vitally important because information about the financial health of a ministry is often based on the information contained in such reports. Unfortunately, this area has not received a great deal of attention in the past and, in fact, has been frequently neglected. Because the church financial statements are considered key documents, certain common characteristics should be present in these statements. Robert Gray, in his instructive work *Managing the Church*, makes the following recommendations:[9]

- They should be easily understood so that any member of the church who takes the time to study them will understand what they are saying. (This is the one characteristic that is the most frequently absent.)
- They should be concise so that the person studying them will not get lost in detail.
- They should be all-inclusive and should embrace all activities of the church, such as church schools, summer camp, and so on. If there are two or three funds, the statement should clearly show the relationship between the funds without a lot of confusing detail.
- They should have a focal point for comparison. In most instances, this will be a comparison with the budget or figures from the corresponding period last year.
- They should be prepared on a timely basis. The longer the delay after the end of the period, the longer the time before corrective action can be taken.

Actually, these features could be applied to almost any type of business enterprise. (Unfortunately, most financial statements presented in churches follow the lines of inertia or tradition—"We've always done it that way!" A frequent problem is that the individual involved simply doesn't know what to do or how to do it.)

One of the most frequent problems is that the volunteer engaged in financial responsibilities (doing the job on a part-time basis) does not have the time or the training to develop new or improved ways of presenting things, even if it would greatly benefit the church. Also, there is mixed reluctance on the part of the nonaccountant to make changes in financial statement formats because he lacks confidence in his ability to tinker with the "mysteries" of accounting. Furthermore, "just about the time the treasurer is really becoming familiar with church statements and could start to make meaningful changes, his term expires and he is replaced with someone else who has to start from scratch."[10]

One answer, then, is to develop a basic format and stay with it. Some financial reports are shown in Exhibits 5–5, 5–6, and 5–7. These examples aren't necessarily the final word in reports. Therefore, choose a format that suits your needs, or modify one of

9. Robert N. Gray, *Managing the Church* (New York: NCC Publication Services, 1977), 2:124.
10. Ibid., 2:124–25.

those provided in the exhibits. The actual statements to be used would vary depending on the type of information desired and the size of the ministry involved. One of the greatest contributions the treasurer can make is the development of an effective form of financial reporting so that the reports are understandable and meaningful to the reader.

Professional Advice

Many churches cannot afford outside accounting professionals. However, good resource people are usually available either within the congregation or certainly within the community. If you cannot afford to hire outside individuals to help you on a regular basis, at least use them as a reference when questions arise.

Annual Audit

The financial records of every church should be audited periodically. This is true whether the church is small or large. The basis for the audit is not a suspicion of incompetence or wrongdoing, nor should it be looked upon as an indication of distrust or a lack of confidence in those people handling funds. On the contrary, an audit is an honest, objective, and impersonal evaluation of the church's financial systems and procedures and its financial statements.

A complete audit should result in the detection of errors, deficiencies in certain policies, and gaps in procedures, whether intentional or through carelessness. It should also result in some type of formal recommendations to the church leadership as to areas where improvement in the church's procedures can be made. There are at least five advantages of an audit:

1. It helps to improve the church's financial reporting systems, procedures, and internal control.
2. It can result in suggestions for improvement of systems and procedures.
3. It can help a church avoid potential financial and legal problems.
4. It can result in improved church operations.
5. It provides assurance to the congregation and outsiders that the church's financial records are being properly maintained.

In those churches where the cost of an audit is prohibitive, the books should at least be examined by an audit committee appointed by the church from its membership. In many cases, the audit committee may consist of the finance committee, except for the elimination of the treasurer and financial secretary. The treasurer and financial secretary should be present when the audit is performed in order to locate items and to explain areas that are in question. They should not, however, be a part of the audit committee or have any responsibility directly related to it.

Normally, the audit should be conducted as soon as possible after the close of the fiscal year. After a time has been arranged, the financial secretary and treasurer should bring the records and supporting data to the committee for the audit.

The key phrase once again is internal control. When talking to an auditor or the audit committee, you should especially direct their attention to areas that are unusual or complex and where their expertise is needed or can be beneficial.

In selecting an auditor, try to look for a person or firm that either specializes in, or has experience in dealing with, nonprofit organizations.

Establishing a Fiscal Year

The setting of a fiscal year doesn't always have to coincide with the calendar year. The fiscal year should correspond with the organization's natural operating cycle. Aside from the common practice of adhering to the calendar year, there are at least two other possible alternatives:

1. A fiscal year that begins October 1 and ends September 30 can flow concurrently with the fall programming of the church. Furthermore, if your church conducts an annual pledge campaign, the best time to embark upon this drive would be in the fall, not during January when Christmas bills are being dealt with.

2. July 1 is another option, particularly for a large church. If an audit is conducted each year, July is a good time to start the process, while activity is low. It also frees staff people to close the books, prepare for the audit, and be ready for the increased church activities that pick up in the fall. Frequently, some accounting firms offer favorable rates for work performed during the summer months.

Conclusion

Well, there it is! I trust you have been either stimulated to make some improvements in your financial procedures or convinced even more that your fiscal house is in order. Whatever your situation, if you prove to be faithful in the handling of money, God will entrust you with even greater things.

"If you have not been faithful in the use of unrighteous mammon, who will entrust the true riches to you?" (Luke 16:11).

Exhibit 5–1
Summary of Receipts

SUMMARY OF RECEIPTS

DATE _____

OFFERING _____

ENVELOPES:

    GENERAL FUND $ _____

    MISSION FUND   _____

    BUILDING FUND   _____

    _____   _____

    _____   _____

TOTAL ENVELOPES   _____

    LOOSE   _____

GRAND TOTAL DEPOSITED   _____

COUNTED BY: _____

_____

_____

Exhibit 5–2
Giving Envelopes

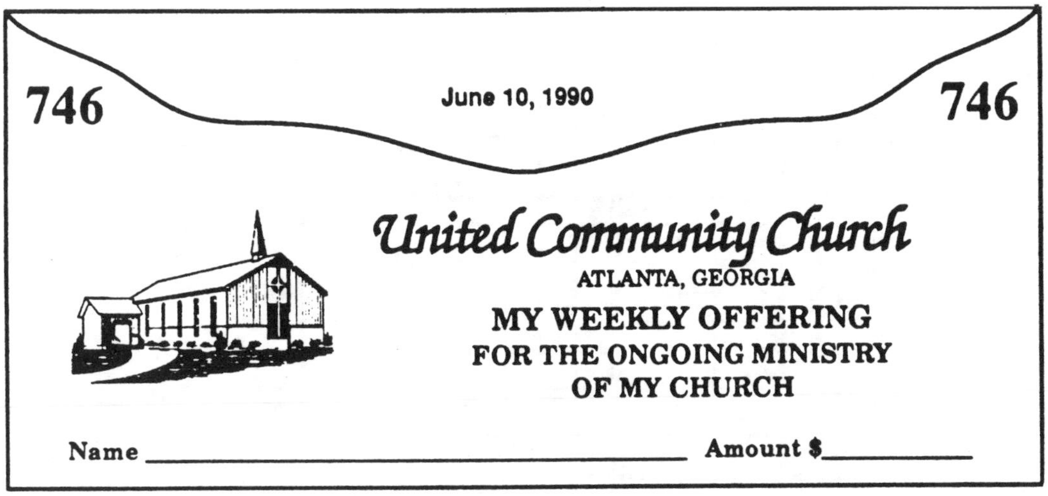

746   June 10, 1990   746

United Community Church
ATLANTA, GEORGIA
MY WEEKLY OFFERING
FOR THE ONGOING MINISTRY
OF MY CHURCH

Name _____ Amount $_____

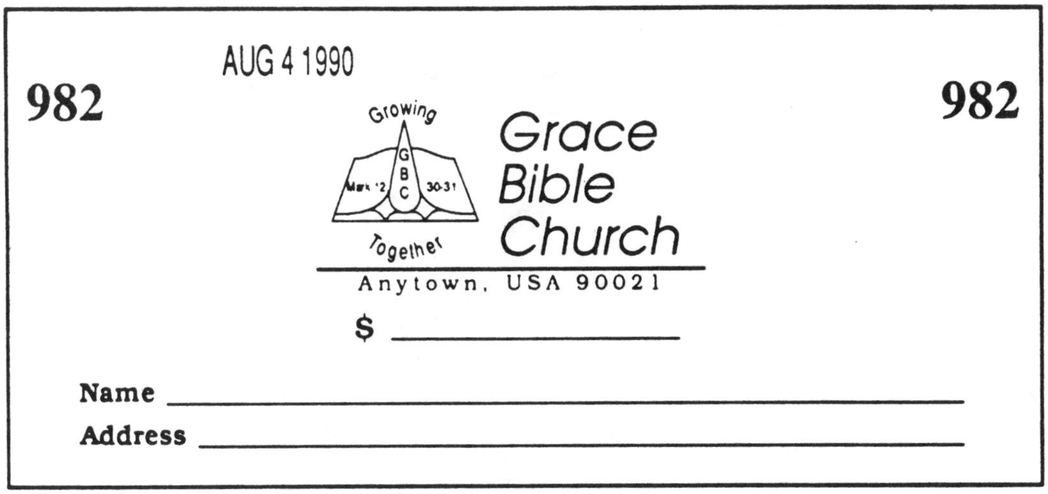

AUG 4 1990

982   982

Growing
GBC
Mark 2   30-31
Together

Grace Bible Church

Anytown, USA 90021

$ _____

Name _____
Address _____

311   311

Thanksgiving

Amount $ _____

Name _____

Exhibit 5–3
Cash Receipts Journal

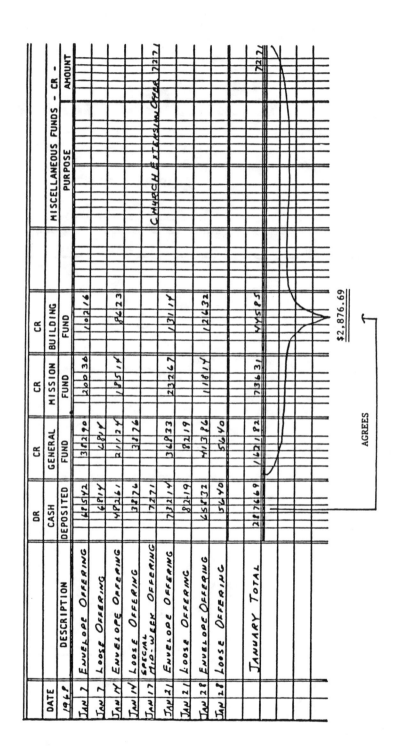

DATE 1966	DESCRIPTION	DR CASH DEPOSITED	CR GENERAL FUND	CR MISSION FUND	CR BUILDING FUND		MISCELLANEOUS FUNDS – CR –	
							PURPOSE	AMOUNT
Jan 7	Envelope Offering	615.42	362.90	200.36	102.16			
Jan 7	Loose Offering	68.14	68.14					
Jan 14	Envelope Offering	483.61	311.24	105.14	86.23			
Jan 14	Loose Offering	38.76	38.76					
Jan 17	Special Mid-Week Offering	72.71					Church Extension Coor.	72.71
Jan 21	Envelope Offering	732.14	368.33	232.67	131.14			
Jan 21	Loose Offering	82.19	82.19					
Jan 28	Envelope Offering	658.32	413.86	118.14	126.32			
Jan 28	Loose Offering	56.40	56.40					
	JANUARY TOTAL	2876.69	1621.82	736.31	445.85			72.71

AGREES

$2,876.69

Exhibit 5–4
Suggested Chart of Accounts

FIRST CHRISTIAN CHURCH

Receipts

General Fund
301 Envelope Offerings
302 Loose Offerings
308 Interest on Savings Accounts
309 Miscellaneous Income

Mission Fund
321 Envelope Offerings
322 Special Offerings
329 Miscellaneous Income

Building Fund
341 Envelope Offerings
342 Special Offerings
349 Miscellaneous Income

Special Funds
361 Offerings
362 Special Gifts
363 Memorial Gifts
369 Miscellaneous Income

Disbursements

General Fund

Physical Plant
401 Heat
402 Utilities
403 Custodian Salaries
404 Social Security Tax
405 Janitorial Supplies
406 Insurance
407 Repair and Maintenance - Building and Grounds
408 Repair and Maintenance - Equipment

409   Telephone
410   Equipment
411   Bus Expense
412   Miscellaneous

Pastoral Ministry
421   Salary
422   Literature and Printing
423   Office Supplies
424   Pulpit Supply
425   Special Meetings Expense
426   Parsonage - Insurance
427   Pension Plan
428   Special Travel Allowances
429   Auto Allowance
430   Parsonage Utilities

Christian Education
441   Salary
442   Literature and Printing
443   Office Supplies
444   Pension Plan
445   Special Travel Allowances
446   Auto Allowance
447   Utilities Allowance

Worship Service
461   Music and Choir Expense
462   Literature and Printing
463   Office Supplies
464   Flowers

Miscellaneous General Expense
481   Special Gifts
482   Advertising
483   Office Salaries

484 Social Security Tax
485 Flowers
486 Miscellaneous

Mission Fund

501 North American Baptist General Conference
502
(an account would be established and assigned an account number for each organization or person for which mission support is budgeted)

Building Fund

601 Construction Projects
602
(an account would be established and assigned an account number for each project)
621 Interest Expense
622 Principal Payments

Special Funds

701 Library Fund, etc.
(a separate account would be established for each fund which will not liquidate itself immediately)
721 Special Offerings
722 Special Gifts
723 Memorial Gifts

Exhibit 5–5
Financial Report Samples

FIRST CHURCH
Any Town, Any State

CASH RECONCILIATION
Year Ended December 31, 1969

	General Fund	Mission Fund	Building Fund	Special Funds	Total
Cash Balance - January 1, 1969					
National Bank - checking account	$ 1,242.16	$ - 0 -	$ 232.10	$ 864.32	$ 2,338
Savings account	- 0 -	- 0 -	5,000.00	- 0 -	5,000
Total Cash on Hand January 1, 1969	$ 1,242.16	$ - 0 -	$ 5,232.10	$ 864.32	$ 7,338
Cash Received During the Year	$24,114.10	$16,400.43	$10,382.16	$ 1,003.86	$51,900
Total Cash to Account For	$25,356.26	$16,400.43	$15,614.26	$ 1,868.18	$59,239
Cash Disbursed During the Year	24,073.14	16,400.43	9,882.41	1,222.26	51,578
Cash Balance - December 31, 1969	$ 1,283.12	$ - 0 -	$ 5,731.85	$ 645.92	$ 7,660
Made Up as Follows:					
National Bank - checking account	$ 1,283.12	$ - 0 -	$ 731.85	$ 645.92	$ 2,660
Savings account	- 0 -	- 0 -	5,000.00	- 0 -	5,000
Total Cash on Hand December 31, 1969	$ 1,283.12	$ - 0 -	$ 5,731.85	$ 645.92	$ 7,660

Exhibit 5–6
Financial Report Samples

FIRST CHURCH
Any Town, Any State

GENERAL FUND DISBURSEMENTS
Year Ended December 31, 1969

Disbursements - General Fund	Budget	Actual	Over (Short)
Physical Plant:			
Utilities	$ 2,100.00	$ 2,069.14	$ (30.86)
Custodian salaries	3,200.00	3,200.00	- 0 -
Janitor supplies	270.00	232.14	(37.86)
Insurance	830.00	826.40	(3.60)
Repairs and maintenance	200.00	360.40	160.40
Equipment purchased	300.00	46.00	(254.00)
Bus expense	260.00	323.95	63.95 —
Miscellaneous	140.00	111.12	(28.88)
Total Physical Plant	$ 7,300.00	$ 7,169.15	$ (130.85)
Pastoral Ministry:			
Salary, housing allowance	$ 8,600.00	$ 8,600.00	- 0 -
Literature and printing	100.00	156.43	56.43 —
Office supplies	100.00	96.32	(3.68)
Pulpit supply	100.00	160.00	60.00 —
Pension plan - (10-12% approximately)	900.00	900.00	- 0 -
Auto allowance	900.00	900.00	- 0 -
Special travel allowances	150.00	317.32	167.32 —
Total Pastoral Ministry	$10,850.00	$11,130.07	$ 280.07
Christian Education:			
Salary	$ 1,800.00	$ 1,800.00	$ - 0 -
Literature and printing	50.00	13.08	(36.92)
Office supplies	50.00	16.09	(33.91)
Auto allowance	600.00	600.00	- 0 -
Total Christian Education	$ 2,500.00	$ 2,429.17	$ (70.83)
Worship and Service:			
Music and choir expense	$ 460.00	$ 432.16	$ (27.84)
Literature and printing	590.00	369.27	(220.73)
Office supplies	90.00	118.49	28.49
Flowers	60.00	62.42	2.42
Total Worship and Service	$ 1,200.00	$ 982.34	$ (217.66)

Exhibit 5–7
Financial Report Samples

FIRST CHURCH
Any Town, Any State

GENERAL FUND RECEIPTS
Year Ended December 31, 1969

Receipts - General Fund	Budget	Actual	Over (Short)
Envelope offerings	$23,000.00	$22,294.89	$ (705.11)
Loose offerings	1,400.00	1,764.21	364.21
Miscellaneous income	60.00	55.00	(5.00)
Total Receipts	$24,460.00	$24,114.10	$ (345.90)
Percent Short of Budget			1.5%

Chapter 6

The Fundamentals of Budgeting

He who is slack in his work
Is brother to him who destroys.

Proverbs 18:9

Who needs a budget?" someone might ask. "Let's just spend money as the Lord provides. If God is in it, He will supply!" One prominent pastor said, "Budgets limit God." But do they? Does a budget really stifle the work of the Holy Spirit in the local church?

The reality of the issue is that, for a church to be successful in managing its financial resources, budgets are an absolute necessity. Although most people in church leadership recognize this fact, many consider budgets a necessary evil. That's usually because the perception or philosophy behind budgeting isn't clearly understood. Often budgets are viewed as merely a method of exercising financial restraint and control—they have a negative connotation.

Budgets when viewed properly are control mechanisms. But, more than that, they are a planning tool and an operational guide to help the local church achieve its short- and long-range objectives. Webster defines a budget as "an estimate of future financial income and outgo." As cold and as sterile as that may sound, church financial officers should view it as an opportunity to look ahead—to make plans.

The budget doesn't dictate what is to be done; it is supposed to conform to *your* plans. You are in control! Luke 14:28 tells us that before a man builds a tower, he sits down and counts the cost. You need to decide if you actually need to build a "tower" in the first place. Simply because you can afford to build, add staff, enlarge the worship center, start a day school, or whatever the endeavor, counting the cost should include maintenance of the "tower" or support expenses for these new projects.

The point is, decide ahead of time what you want to do. Once you feel sure of your need, ask yourself, "Can we afford this now? What about six months from now, when we have to hire an additional tower janitor? What about heating and lighting the tower?" This additional planning isn't supposed to discourage you in what you believe God would have you to do. But counting the cost means counting *all* the conceivable costs—both current and future.

Simply stated, plan carefully first, budget second.

The Overview Process

An effective budgeting process requires two important elements.

Looking Back

Past giving patterns are important in helping you determine whether you can afford to fund what you believe is needed. This information can often demonstrate past trends relating to spending, expenses, and costs connected with ministry thrusts (i.e., building programs, missions emphasis). For instance, in the area of giving, how much have offerings increased over the last three years? Can you expect this trend to continue? Why? You will have to do your homework in this area to arrive at usable figures. However, by using records from the past (canceled checks, bankbooks, ledgers, or other financial records), you can develop a simple profile of past performance. (See Exhibit 6–1.)

Looking Ahead

Budgets or projections are plans expressed in numbers—they are future needs set to figures. Since budgets are customarily designed to accommodate a twelve-month period, long-range plans must be accounted for in the process, lest, as our passage in Luke points out, "when he has laid a foundation, and is not able to finish, all who observe it begin to ridicule him."

Goals for your church are essential to good budgeting. A pastor was overheard to have said, "We prepare a budget every year but practically abandon it after six months because things tend to change so much." That is a result of poor planning or making a budget so tight and restrictive that unforeseen events are not accounted for. Therefore, in your planning process, allow for the unexpected by setting aside funds into contingency accounts. That too is a part of planning ahead!

The formation of a planning group to establish goals for the next one to three years is extremely important. Budgeting should not consist simply of adding 10 percent across-the-board to last year's budget. Ask yourself, "Where are we now, and where do we want to go?"

Additionally, determine, to the best of your ability, what the local economy will be like in the next twelve months. There are several sources you can turn to for this information. Many large banks produce an annual, local economic outlook report. State and city governments also have their own "educated guesses" of future economic conditions available. They too need to plan their budgets based on expected "contributions"—taxes.

Finally, the question of whether your congregation can handle an increase in their financial commitment needs to be addressed. Perhaps a 10 percent increase in the church budget would realistically exceed the ability of the people to meet that requirement.

There are those who would argue that people need to be "stretched," to "step out on faith," to be challenged. However, church leaders need to keep in mind that there is a fine line between faith and presumption. Many churches "write checks" and then ask God to "cash" them. Often a church that wants to undertake a project will go ahead and put it in the budget—a "faith budget"—even though it may require a 15 percent increase in giving over the next year, when in fact, the giving has been increasing only 6 percent for the last three years.

The scenario here is all too common. The pastor will have the task of convincing the people that they need to increase their giving to meet the new budget. This results in more "pulpit time" being devoted to the subject of money and budgets, especially if giving falls short of the projections. Also, if the budgeted items are purchased, a cash flow shortage develops, which in turn puts more pressure on the congregation. The next logical step is to cut back ongoing ministries in order to pay the bills already incurred for the new project.

Without a question, there certainly is a place for faith when it comes to giving. However, the faith challenge needs to be realistic and within the capability of a local congregation to meet the need. That is why looking back at past performance and then looking ahead with an understanding of the basic economic factors that affect giving will go a long way toward producing a budget that will allow people to both *stretch* and *reach* the goal.

The Production Process

Many aspiring young preachers have been given the K.I.S.S. principle—the polite spelled-out version of which is "Keep It Simple, Saint!" That's good advice for those preparing an annual budget as well. Make the budget simple and easy to understand. Even if the church is large, the projections can still be kept in elementary terms and understandable to the average church member. It doesn't matter how big your church is; the basic format can still be the same.

First Step—Departments

Reduce the entire church structure into departments (i.e., Music, Youth, Facilities). Each area of ministry is to be assigned either a staff person, if the church is large, or a layperson. This individual is responsible for projecting the income, if there is any, and the expense portion of the budget.

Second Step—Line-Items

Each department should have "line-items" assigned to the revenue and expense portion of the budget. This means that every conceivable type of expense should have a category and be placed within the budget. For example, Youth Ministry could have a separate line entry labeled "Publications and Materials" for items such as quarterlies, Sunday school papers, maps, and songbooks. When several items are similar, they can be grouped together under a single line-item. Using Youth Ministry as an example, you might place Publications and Materials in with Equipment (such as slide projectors and visual aids) and title them both as "Teaching Aids" or "Material and Equipment." If the church is quite small, simply put all youth-related expenses under one heading—Youth.

The line-item method allows you the freedom to be as detailed as you choose. You can plan for and track any segment of the church budget you desire. A word of caution though—don't get too general and lump everything together into as few categories as possible. That only defeats the purpose of planning and control.

The point is, every expected expense should be placed into a department line-item. This will prevent funds or expenses from "falling through the cracks."

Third Step—Revenue and Expense

If you expect to charge a fee for an item or event, list it as both a revenue *and* expense item. It is important to plan for money coming in as well as for those funds being spent.

Fourth Step—Chart of Accounts

Assign numbers to your departments and line-items. The listing of these numbers is commonly called a chart of accounts. (See chapter 5 and Exhibit 5–4.)

Format—Large Church

The format for a large church may look like Exhibit 6–2.

Format—Smaller Church

A smaller church may want to a follow a simpler, more general format. Exhibit 6–3 shows a basic, simple budget that can be expanded by adding more line-items. The sample can also be reduced by grouping all similar line-items into one line-item. For example, a smaller church would have one line-item for salaries and expenses instead of breaking this category out by department as is the case in a larger church. This example is only an aid, and you should not hesitate to make changes where they are appropriate.

Worksheets

Worksheets can also be helpful in the preliminary steps of gathering data and then summarizing the budget information. Sample worksheets are presented in Exhibits 6–4, 6–5, 6–6, and 6–7. Department heads, as well as members of the Finance Committee, will find these useful.

Although the first time you prepare a budget using these methods may require a lot of effort, the next time will be much simpler. Even though using this new procedure could result in many more line-item entries than you had in past budgets, it will still be easier to track income and expenses with the department/line-item method.

The Presentation Process

There is one thing you want to avoid in presenting budgets to the church leadership or to the congregation—surprises! An open and honest approach will avoid suspicion and a confrontational atmosphere. How do you accomplish this? By adopting a "flow of cooperation" within the entire organization. The process is as follows.

The Assembly Line

The department heads assemble their own projections based on past experience, plus what they feel will be needed to carry on the ministry in their specific area. The purpose is to include the people who have the responsibility of overseeing their particular ministry in the budgeting process.

With an autocratic or nonparticipative organization, be it a church or a business, top management sets the budgets, issues them to "operations managers," and then holds the managers accountable for meeting them. The organization managers (department heads) must then work within the budgetary guidelines to meet their stated goals. On the other hand, with participative budgeting, department heads submit individual budgets. Top management analyzes the projections using some of the techniques mentioned earlier. They also discuss and modify those budgets (when necessary, with the participation of department heads) and combine them into the overall budget.

Therefore, for budgeting to be effectively used as a *coordinating* tool, it must be a participative system. When all the people who are responsible for managing the finances of their ministry are allowed to participate in the budget preparation process, the entire organization can benefit. Estimates of what the church can achieve the next year, and at what cost, are usually more realistic with a participative system than if those at the top make the projections alone.

However, it must be remembered that department heads participating in the budgeting process will no doubt place their own personal desires for their ministry as a priority. These personal goals cannot be allowed to be the primary motivation for their projections. A church must make sure that the goals of the department heads and those of the church can be reached simultaneously. If this relationship is not clear, department heads might be tempted to inflate their projections at the expense of the overall church objectives.

Advantages of a participative budget include:

- Improved initiative, morale, and enthusiasm
- A more realistic budget plan
- Properly delegated responsibility that is more readily accepted
- Increased interdepartmental cooperation
- A higher degree of awareness at all levels
- A sense of "ownership" of the entire budget and not just a special-interest area

The most effective budgets are those that originate at the bottom of the organizational ladder. This bottom-up approach is the key element that leads to accuracy, relevance, and the ultimate success of the budget. The actual procedures used in budget development and the end uses of the budget are equally important.

Inspectors

After a first-draft proposal has been submitted from the departments, the budget goes to a Finance Committee. This group of individuals, who are *not* department heads, reviews the soundness of the submitted budgets as a whole. It is this committee's job to determine if the church can, in fact, meet the projections. This evaluation, as mentioned before, is based on the local economy, past giving patterns, and an assessment of the members' ability to support the new budget.

If the projections are beyond what the Finance Committee believes to be attainable, then the budgets are returned to the department heads with suggestions for reductions, and they may take appropriate action. Again, the goal is cooperation through participation. If specific cuts can be made, then they need to be made by the departments and not the Finance Committee. If all the departments cannot reduce their budgets to a satisfactory level, then the pastor needs to be informed. He may decide to go to the congregation, after the budget is approved in its present form, and challenge them to a greater financial commitment. However, if the senior pastor doesn't wish to do this, then the Finance Committee may have to make the needed reductions to balance the budget. Any cuts that are made at this point must be clearly within the guidelines of the stated priorities of the church. They may be in specific departments or across-the-board cuts, the decision being the Finance Committee's.

The Rollout

Once approved by the Finance Committee, the budget goes to the church's ruling board for acceptance. If a congregational vote is required, now is the time to call a special budget meeting, with every interested church member invited to attend. The purpose of this meeting is for information only, sort of an open forum. It is not intended to be a time for final adoption of the budget. Hopefully, once all the questions and issues have been satisfactorily dealt with, the general congregational meeting can convene the next week. At this meeting, the budget can then be approved by the people. This is merely an opportunity for questions and answers. If there is someone who has a question about a specific item and a point of clarification would be long and involved, speak with this person during the following week—if possible on a one-to-one basis. Make every effort, though, to move the process along, avoiding debates and confrontations. (See Exhibit 6–8.)

Conclusion

Although blank sample budget forms listing general categories and line-items are presented in Exhibit 6–5, it is the general format that is always important. Church leaders and congregations generally want to know the following information:

1. What was our giving last year?
2. What was last year's budget?
3. Did we accomplish the projections or miss them? By how much?
4. What is the projected giving for the new budget year?
5. What is the new budget?
6. What are the major categories?
7. Do the leaders expect us to achieve our goal?

The budget can illustrate all these points in whatever form you choose. You can use a formal line-item budget, pie charts, graphs, or even a narrative summary. There is no hard, fast rule when it comes to illustrating a budget. Again, I would suggest that it be kept simple.

One last principle: Don't allow budgets to be the absolute final word. Conditions can change, and it may be necessary to increase or decrease projections. Maybe it would be best to move some of the line-items around to adapt to present conditions. The point is, don't allow the ministry of the church to become a slave to the numbers in the budget. The tail shouldn't wag the dog! As stated earlier, the budget is simply a road map, but don't take too many detours.

"All things must be done properly and in an orderly manner," the Bible tells us (1 Corinthians 14:40)—good advice, particularly when applied to the area of church budgets. To insure a smooth and orderly process, those entrusted with the responsibility of preparing the budget must do their homework. The presentation should be accurate, simple, and meaningful. The annual budget meeting should be a time of festiveness, not fighting, and caring instead of quarreling.

All in favor, say, "Aye!"

Exhibit 6–1
Income for Last Five Years Record

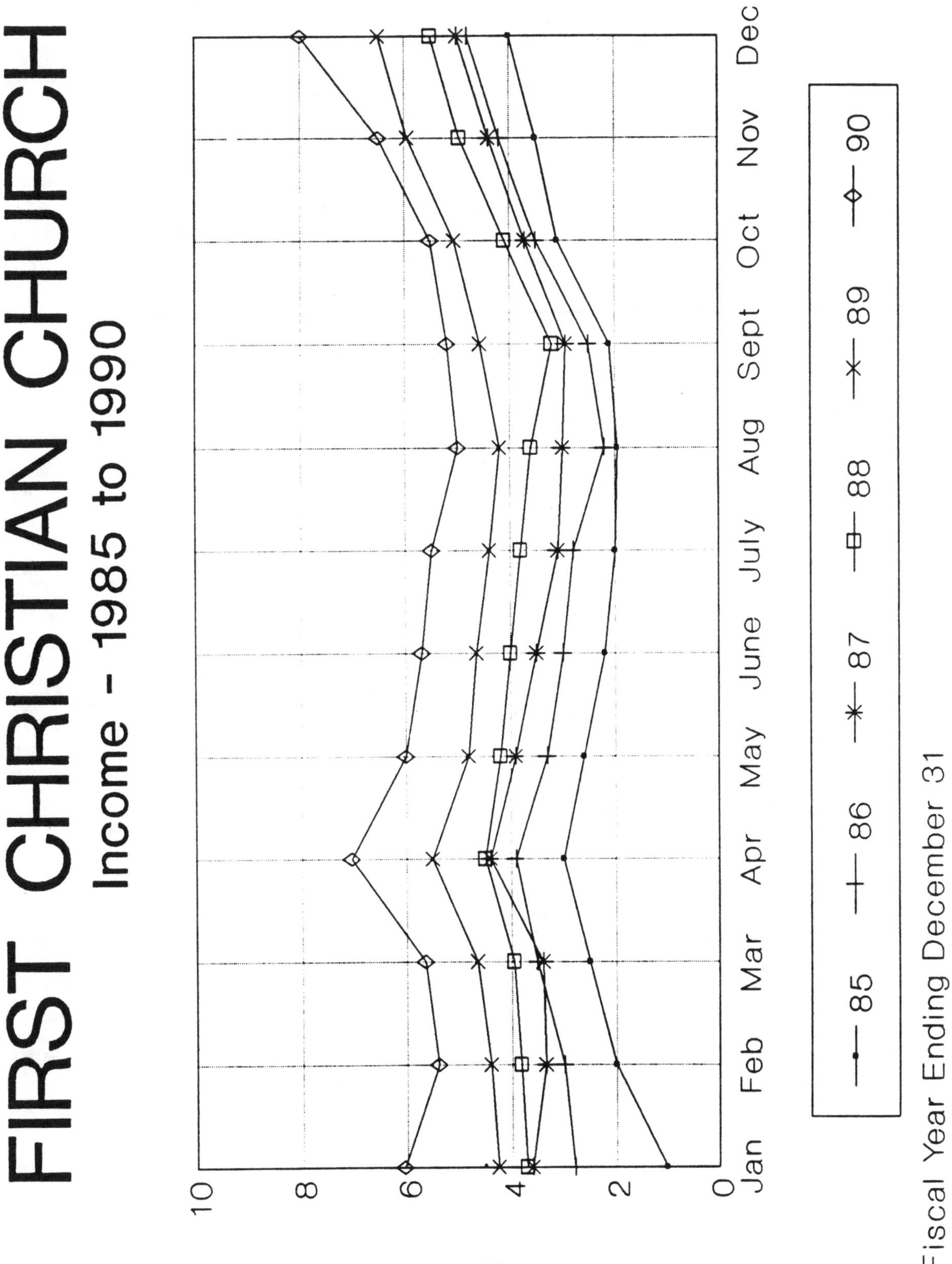
FIRST CHRISTIAN CHURCH
Income - 1985 to 1990
10
8
6
4
2
0
Jan
Feb
Mar
Apr
May
June
July
Aug
Sept
Oct
Nov
Dec
85
86
87
88
89
90
Fiscal Year Ending December 31

Exhibit 6–2
Youth Department Annual Budget Sample

The format for a large church may look like this:

YOUTH DEPARTMENT - #202

Annual Budget

		<u>1986</u> <u>Actual</u>	<u>1987</u> <u>Projected</u>
	<u>Revenue</u>		
3322	Camps	----------	----------
	<u>Total</u> <u>Revenue</u>	----------	----------
	<u>Expenses</u>		
6202	Pastor's Salary	000000	000000
6203	Secretary's Salary	000000	000000
6204	Employee Expenses	000000	000000
6205	Camps	000000	000000
6206	Curriculum	000000	000000
6207			
6208			
6209			
6210			
<u>Total</u> <u>Expenses</u>		000000	000000
<u>Total</u> <u>Less</u> <u>Revenue</u>		000000	000000

Exhibit 6–3
Christian Education Annual Budget Sample

A smaller church may want to a follow a simpler, more general format:

CHRISTIAN EDUCATION - #200

Annual Budget

		1986 Actual	1987 Projected
	Revenue		
3322	Camps	----------	----------
3352	Banquets	----------	----------
	Total Revenue	----------	----------
	Expenses		
4412	Salaries & Expenses	000000	000000
4422	Literature & Printing	000000	000000
2282	Camps	000000	000000
4572	Banquets	000000	000000
4485			
4490			
4495			
Total Expenses		000000	000000
Total Less Revenue		000000	000000

Exhibit 6-4
Church Annual Budget Sample

FIRST CHURCH - ANNUAL BUDGET - 1987

:===

RECEIPTS	1986	Proposed 1987	Difference (+ or -)

General Offerings
:=================================== ============ ========= ===========

		1986	Proposed 1987	Difference
4100	General Offerings	95000	105000	10000
4150	Interest of Savings Acct	500	500	0
4200	Miscellaneous Income	300	300	0
Total General Offerings		95800	105800	10000

Designated Receipts
:=================================== ============ ========= ===========

		1986	Proposed 1987	Difference
3100	Missions	12000	13200	1200
3150	Organ Fund	500	500	0
3250	Debt Retirement	12000	12000	0
3300	Camps	1000	1100	100
3350	Banquets	1000	1000	0
3400	Other	75	75	0
Total Designated Offerings		26575	27875	1300

TOTAL RECEIPTS	122375	133675	11300

DISBURSEMENTS

Physical Plant

		1986	Proposed 1987	Difference
4010	Heat	4000	4500	500
4020	Utilities	2500	3300	800
4030	Custodial Services	4400	4600	200
4040	Social Security Taxes	485	514	29
4050	Janitorial Supplies	300	325	25
4060	Insurance	1200	1250	50
4070	Repair & Maintenance	2000	2000	0
4080	Repair & Maint -Equip	1000	1000	0
4090	Telephone	3000	3500	500
4100	Equipment	500	500	0
4110	Bus Expense	1500	1700	200
4120	Miscellaneous	100	100	0
Total Physical Plant		20985	23289	2304

```
Christian Education
------------------------------
4410    Salary (All Pastors)      45000      47700      2700
4420    Literature & Print          600        650        50
4430    Office Supplies             200        215        15
4440    Pension Plan               1200       1250        50
4450    Special Travel Allowance    500        500         0
4470    Camps                      1200       1400       200
------------------------------   ----------   --------  ---------
Total Christian Education        48700      51715      3015


Worship Service
------------------------------
4610    Music & Choir Expense       900        950        50
4620    Literature & Printing      1200       1250        50
4630    Office Supplies             500        500         0
4640    Flowers                    1500       1600         0
------------------------------   ----------   --------  ---------
Total Worship Service            4100       4300       100


Misc. General Expense
------------------------------
4810    Special Gifts               300        300         0
4820    Advertising                 300        325        25
4830    Office Salaries           20000      22000      2000
4840    Social Security Tax        1440       1515        75
4850    Banquets                    300        300         0
4860    Miscellaneous               500        500         0
------------------------------   ---------    --------  ---------
Total Misc Gen Expense           22840      24940       2100


Missions Expense
------------------------------
5010 No. American Mission Conf     8000       9000       1000
5020 Any org. or individual        3000       3500        500
------------------------------   ----------   --------  ---------
Total Mission Expense            11000      12500       1500


Building Fund
------------------------------
6010    Construction Projects      3000       3000         0
6020       (each project would be given a line-item)       0
6210    Interest Expense           1200       1200         0
6220    Principle Payments        12000      12000         0
------------------------------   ----------   --------  ---------
Total Building Fund              16200      16200        0


=================================   ===========  ========= ===========
TOTAL DISBURSEMENTS              123825     132944      9019

=================================   ===========  ========= ===========
SURPLUS OR DEFICIT                -1450        731       2281
```

99

Exhibit 6–5
Sample Budget Form

		Current	Proposed
I. World Missions Ministries			
Cooperative Program		_____	_____
Associational Missions		_____	_____
Direct Missions		_____	_____
Children's Home		_____	_____
Local Missions		_____	_____
	Total	_____	_____
II. Pastoral Ministries			
Pastor's Salary		_____	_____
Housing & Utilities		_____	_____
Associate Pastor's Salary		_____	_____
Housing & Utilities		_____	_____
Secretary		_____	_____
Radio & Television		_____	_____
Deacon Care Program		_____	_____
Revival		_____	_____
	Total	_____	_____
III. Education Ministries			
Minister of Education's Salary		_____	_____
Housing & Utilities		_____	_____
Secretary		_____	_____
Sunday School		_____	_____
Church Training		_____	_____
Brotherhood		_____	_____
Woman's Missionary Union		_____	_____
Leadership Training		_____	_____
	Total	_____	_____
IV. Music and Worship Ministries			
Minister of Music's Salary		_____	_____
Housing & Utilities		_____	_____
Organist's Salary		_____	_____
Music & Supplies		_____	_____
Special Programs		_____	_____
Worship Supplies		_____	_____
	Total	_____	_____

Budget Worksheets from *Church Administration Handbook*, edited by Bruce Powers. Chapter entitled *Financial Procedures* by Mark Short, Broadman Press, Nashville, Tennessee. Copyright 1985.

V. Support Ministries

V. Support Ministries
 Library   _____   _____
 Recreation   _____   _____
 Church Secretary's Salary   _____   _____
 Office Supplies/Postage   _____   _____
 Stewardship/Budget Development   _____   _____
 Auditing/Financial Records   _____   _____
 Travel Expense (all staff)   _____   _____
 Convention expense (all staff)   _____   _____
 Annuity Payments   _____   _____
 Social Security   _____   _____
 Special Events   _____   _____
 Kitchen operation/supplies   _____   _____
        Total   _____   _____

VI. Buildings and Grounds
 Janitor's Salary   _____   _____
 Utilities   _____   _____
 Insurance   _____   _____
 Repairs   _____   _____
 Taxes   _____   _____
 Supplies   _____   _____
 Debt Retirement   _____   _____
 New Facilities   _____   _____
        Total   _____   _____

Summary by Categories

 I. World Missions Ministries   _____   _____
 II. Pastoral Ministries   _____   _____
 III. Education Ministries   _____   _____
 IV. Music and Worship Ministries   _____   _____
 V. Support Ministries   _____   _____
 VI. Buildings and Grounds   _____   _____
       Grand Total   _____   _____

Exhibit 6–6
Budget Worksheet

	Current Budget-19XX	Actual/Anticipated Totals This Year	Committee Requests	Proposed Budget-19XX
Undesignated Receipts	$_____	$_____	$_____	$_____
DISBURSEMENTS				
Missions				
Cooperative Program	_____	_____	_____	_____
Associational Missions	_____	_____	_____	_____
Local	_____	_____	_____	_____
Total Missions	$_____	$_____	$_____	$_____
Educational Ministry				
Sunday School & Church Training	_____	_____	_____	_____
Vacation Bible School	_____	_____	_____	_____
Woman's Missionary Union	_____	_____	_____	_____
Brotherhood	_____	_____	_____	_____
Youth	_____	_____	_____	_____
Total Education	$_____	$_____	$_____	$_____
Property	$_____	$_____	$_____	$_____
Debt Retirement	$_____	$_____	$_____	$_____
General Operations				
Car Allowances	_____	_____	_____	_____
Conventions	_____	_____	_____	_____
Denominational Retirement	_____	_____	_____	_____
Insurance	_____	_____	_____	_____
Kitchen	_____	_____	_____	_____
Music & Equipment	_____	_____	_____	_____
Office Equipment	_____	_____	_____	_____
Postage	_____	_____	_____	_____
Church Supplies	_____	_____	_____	_____
Payroll Taxes	_____	_____	_____	_____
Utilities	_____	_____	_____	_____
Contingencies	_____	_____	_____	_____
Total General	$_____	$_____	$_____	$_____
Personnel				
Pastor	_____	_____	_____	_____
Church Secretary (part-time)	_____	_____	_____	_____
Janitor (part-time)	_____	_____	_____	_____
Total Personnel	$_____	$_____	$_____	$_____
Total Disbursements	$_____	$_____	$_____	$_____

Exhibit 6–7
Worksheet for Financial Support of the Minister

Worksheet for Financial Support of the Minister

(Duplicate and use a separate sheet for each staff member.)

	This Year	Proposed for Next Year
I. Ministry-Related Expenses		
1. Automobile Allowance	_____	_____
2. Convention Allowance	_____	_____
3. Book Allowance	_____	_____
4. Continuing Education Allowance	_____	_____
5. Hospitality Allowance	_____	_____
TOTAL EXPENSES	_____	_____
II. Protection Benefits		
1. Insurance		
a. Life	_____	_____
b. Long-Term Disability	_____	_____
c. Medical	_____	_____
2. Retirement	_____	_____
TOTAL BENEFITS	_____	_____
III. Basic Compensation Personal Support		
1. Cash Salary	_____	_____
2. Housing Allowance	_____	_____
TOTAL COMPENSATION	_____	_____

Exhibit 6–8
The Budget Production Process

THE PRODUCTION PROCESS

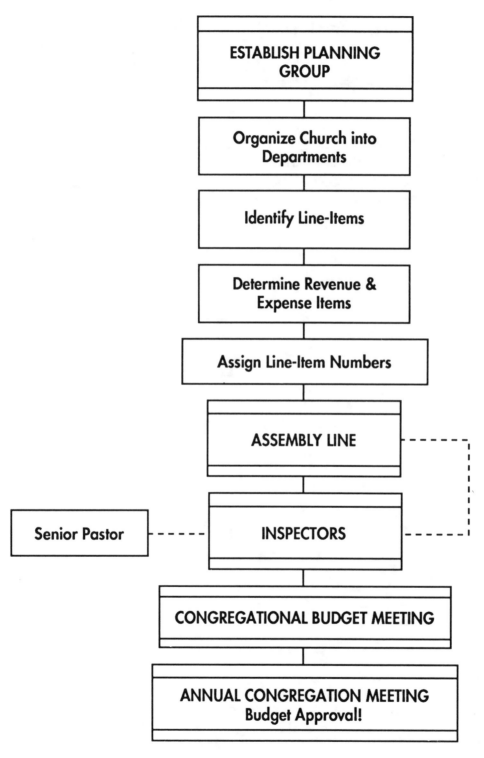

ESTABLISH PLANNING GROUP

Organize Church into Departments

Identify Line-Items

Determine Revenue & Expense Items

Assign Line-Item Numbers

ASSEMBLY LINE

Senior Pastor — — — — INSPECTORS

CONGREGATIONAL BUDGET MEETING

ANNUAL CONGREGATION MEETING
Budget Approval!

Chapter 7

Budgeting and Forecasting— Beyond the Basics

Webster's New World Dictionary defines *status quo* as "the existing state of affairs." All well-managed organizations continually seek for ways to improve their status quo—that is, their existing financial state of affairs. This is accomplished by better regulating costs. Ministries experiencing slow growth implement cost control as a necessity for survival, whereas rapid-growth ministries curb costs to ensure proper allocation of income to support continued success. For both types of ministries, budgeting provides the framework to reduce expenses while deriving the most benefits from available funds.

It's been said before, and it bears repeating, that budgeting ought to be an extension of strategic planning. Managers should scrutinize the business operations of their ministry from a cost-benefit standpoint. That will determine which activities should be reduced or eliminated and which should be given priority to receive more funds. Too often, however, ministries fail to go this extra step. They tend to do things the way they always have in the past, maintaining the status quo. This is not necessarily a criticism, because most churches use volunteer financial people to handle forecasting and budgeting, and it's on a limited basis.

Furthermore, the conventional approach to budgeting often fails. That is because previous budgets are assumed to be a valid base from which to start. But that isn't always true. In order for the budgeting process to be an effective tool, it is necessary to operate with real numbers based on good forecasts. What is needed is the ability to get beyond the basics of the traditional methods of budgeting.

Therefore, the purpose of this brief presentation is threefold: first, to introduce the concept of forecasting; second, to demonstrate a simple but effective way to project income; third, to provide alternatives to the customary, twelve-month, straight-line method of budgeting.

Forecasting

It has been said that forecasting is more art than science. In other words, a good fore-caster "guesses good"! As you prepare a forecast, you should look at as many approaches as possible, consider the trends, new developments, cycles, and anything else that might give you ideas.

One of the toughest forecasting jobs is that of the weather forecaster. Meteorologists observe wind patterns, satellite pictures, air pressure, and years of past trends. Each forecast is based on careful analysis of what is going on, why, and (more important) how it applies to the future. Their forecasts, like those of financial managers, are professional guesses based on knowledge, experience, and common sense. Obviously, we can't consult the Wharton School of Economics, the UCLA Econometric Model, or any other highly developed forecasting method. Even these methods are not 100 percent accurate. Aside from this, the church is a nonprofit corporation, and many of those reports are slanted toward the large corporations, which need high-level, sophisticated data to assist them in making major financial decisions. This information is rooted in theories and studies involving macro- and microeconomics and is beyond the scope of most local churches.

However, there are some basic forecasting tools that we *can* put to use in our local churches. As a start, projecting income is certainly important. After all, what use is an expense budget if the income falls considerably short of the goal? This doesn't mean you lack faith or have "fallen from grace." I've known church leaders who felt they were out of God's will if they did not raise their budget each year. Of course, they always fell short—but that wasn't the point. At least their budget kept increasing! Meanwhile, the pastor had to continually keep asking people to give more money to "meet the budget." And then the people would complain because "the pastor talks about money too much!" That is a common complaint about pastors.

At this point, we need to spend a few moments to examine the practice of forecasting a little more closely. The goal should be to develop a budget that uses real numbers and has meaning.

The Way It Was

Previous giving patterns are helpful in determining whether the present budget is feasible. Past spending shows expenses and costs connected with certain ministry thrusts. For example, what impact did a building or missions emphasis have on giving and expenses? Ask yourself questions. How much have offerings increased over the last few years? Can you expect this trend to continue? If so, why? You will have to do careful research to arrive at usable figures. By using records from the past, you can develop a simple profile of past performance.

Therefore, there are two features to look for when examining past income and expenses:

1. *Trends*. Exhibit 7–1 illustrates highs and lows in past giving patterns. Many giving peaks can be attributable to year-end tax donations, higher attendance at Easter, or other special holiday giving. The low points can be attributed to Christmas holiday bills coming due near the first of the year or to post-year-end, tax-related giving or to the traditional summer slump.

   Expenses should then be accounted for based on past trends. It's simply a question of cash-flow management during the peaks and valleys.

2. *The "X" factor*. Previous financial activity may also reveal what could be called the "X" factor. The "X" might be a major building-fund emphasis that affects cash available for general expenses, or it might be the death or resignation of the senior pastor, a fire, a church split, or any unforeseen problem or factor that significantly affects income.

Back to the Future

Often occurrences outside the realm of the church can seriously impact income and expenses—circumstances we have no control over that still affect the bottom line. Events in the general economy can determine the direction of many of your church's ministries.

For example, a higher inflation rate will affect variable home mortgage rates. For those families with these types of mortgages, less discretionary income will be available. A $100,000 thirty-year mortgage at 10.5 percent interest that increases to 11 percent results in a $450 annual increase. And that is only one-half of 1 percent! The financial leadership of a church needs to keep this in the back of their minds when they hear reports of the "prime rate" going up.

A dramatic increase in the price of oil might affect your church utility expenses. Attendance at services other than on Sunday mornings could drop as gasoline prices increase.

Therefore, some of the more significant aspects to look for in forecasting are economic conditions and new programs that can deflect giving from current needs.

- *Inflation*. People put more money into savings accounts because things cost more; interest rates on savings accounts go up, and uncertainty breeds economic conservativeness.
- *Weather*. Agriculture obviously is impacted when there is a drought, severe cold, or too much rain. Depending on the harvest conditions, giving could rise or drop.
- *Industrial shifts*. Cities with economies tied to certain industries can be seriously

affected by the health of those businesses. Knowing the economic outlook as it relates to the health of these companies would be a wise piece of information to have on hand at forecasting time.

- *A building program*. Generally speaking, a building program will create a deflection away from the general fund. Gifts are often designated to the building fund despite the pastor's encouragement to make this type of giving over and above regular contributions. Experience has shown that this kind of giving—"deflective giving"—can pull anywhere from 18 to 25 percent of funds away from the general needs of the church. Again, a wise forecaster will take this into consideration.

The best forecast combines good, accurate information and management with common sense. Still, forecasting is an uncertain process. However, for a financial manager to ignore past trends or events in the general economy would be shortsighted and foolish.

Once you have the concept of forecasting and many of the details relating to your specific situation available, it is advisable to prepare a *pro forma* accounting statement. A *pro forma* statement is similar to what corporations refer to as a business plan. It's really a model of what the numbers for your church are supposed to look like over the next year (in some cases three years). The *pro forma* statement would be a cash-flow plan—a model of your balance sheet as it would look if the cash flow and future revenues worked out the way you forecasted them.

Forecasting is a significant building block in budgeting for a church. It is an integral part of planning, budgeting, and finance.

Cash Flow Made Simple

Happiness is positive cash flow—at least for a church treasurer. So how can a church increase that happiness? Proper management helps. Since "cash flow" describes how and when money comes into the church and is spent, cash-flow management involves projecting income and expenses with the goal of paying bills on time and creating a surplus for growth.

The Key

Income and expenses are two rather difficult beasts to tame in many churches. So how do we do it? Through forecasting. It's a lot easier to go with the flow when we know where it is going. As already mentioned, the best method is to track giving patterns over the last three years to evaluate the level of revenue and expected changes.

Plotting Income

Use graph paper to draw an income graph for three, overlaid, twelve-month periods (see Exhibit 7–1):

- ✔ Draw a vertical axis (line) and label it "Income."
- ✔ Make the top of the line equal to your total annual giving, and divide the line into equal dollar-amount increments, beginning with $0.
- ✔ Draw a horizontal axis with twelve equally spaced marks to represent the months in each year of the three-year period.
- ✔ Collect income information from the church checkbook, the income journal, or bank deposit slips. These will show when you received money and how much you took in.
- ✔ Plot on the graph the income for the first month.
- ✔ For each successive month, add to the total the income generated that month, and plot the print on the graph.
- ✔ Connect the points to form a line rising from lower left to upper right.
- ✔ At the end of the first year, repeat the process in other colors for the next two years, starting from $0 each time.

Alternative: Use the graphing ability of a computer spreadsheet.

Plotting Expenses

Repeat the graphing process for monthly expenses, using information from your church's checkbook, disbursements journal, or other record of paid bills. Simply add up the expenses for each month, and connect another set of points on the graph.

Looking for Variations

Aside from seasonal patterns (i.e., lower income in the summer), other factors may cause exceptions to the normal flow of giving and expenses. Examples would be a building program that produced a surge in offerings, or a large Christmas pageant that occasioned significant expenses.

What to look for:

- High- and low-income months
- Seasonal periods of greater spending
- Overall trends: Is giving up each year? Plateaued? Falling? How much? Is one year quite different from others? Why?

Projecting Next Year's Graph

Using data from the three-year historical graph, you can form estimates of the coming year's income and expenses. (See Exhibit 7–2.) Note: Expect some variations in the future, just as you found them in the past, but this process will help make a reasonable cash-flow projection.

Finding Trouble Spots

This cash-flow graph provides another important piece of information: the "break-even points," where income and expense lines cross (see Point A in Exhibit 7–2). At these points, you've taken in and spent equal amounts of money. Note: Ideally, both the expense and income lines would travel identical paths on the graph in a continual break-even mode, but this is hardly ever the case. Most churches hope to keep the lines reasonably close, if only at a few given points, being content to break even over time.

What else to look for:

- Negative cash flow: Where the expense line is higher than the income line (see Point B), the church is "in the red"; it has spent more than it has taken in. Note: This isn't always a sign of problems, but it obviously calls for attention and cannot continue indefinitely.
- Positive cash flow: When the income line is on top (see Point C), the church is "in the black"—a comfortable place to be. Positive cash-flow months prepare the church for times when outlays outstrip income.

Key Activity: Keeping your finger on the pulse of cash flow. You need to understand how and when funds come in and go out, paying careful attention to places where the flow is disproportionate in either direction.

Heading Off Trouble

What else can you do about expected cash-flow problems? Here are two suggestions:

Forward-Thinking Budgeting

Create two or three spending plans, because a single budget doesn't always allow for setbacks, unless surpluses are budgeted. Here is how it works. You budget at a certain rate but plan to cut expenses by, say, 10 percent at a specific date if income isn't keeping up with outlays. Some other ideas include:

- Reduce the number of mailings.
- Charge for events that previously were free.
- Delay purchases.

The key element here is that you know that cash flow may be a problem, so the budget includes alternative spending plans to match the income.

Planned Saving and Spending

Almost every church experiences dips in income during summer. A wise cash-flow manager will:

- Set aside a cash reserve during the fat months to cover the lean ones.
- Phase discretional expenditures to take place in high-income months.

Financial Budgets

Every ministry needs to make decisions about where it is going to place its financial resources. The disadvantage a nonprofit organization (a church in particular) has is that it lacks the essential motive to earn a profit. Obviously, it isn't supposed to seek a profit—that isn't the point. In business, however, the profit is a standard, or measuring device, to determine the effectiveness of the company's efforts.

Churches, on the other hand, must have more indirect priorities or diffuse goals. Profit as an ongoing measure of their effectiveness is lost as a tool of management. (That is one of the reasons so many churches are wasteful when it comes to handling money.) Hence, the nonprofit organization must find another method to quantify success, control its operations, evaluate individual performances, and make resource allocation decisions.

A local church requires a specific planning process for setting goals, determining cash spending patterns, and deciding what program services will be provided. These plans should be formulated prior to the annual budget. Many churches traditionally look at how much money they estimate will be available and then look at existing programs to determine if they can afford to continue or increase them. Again, it's sort of a status quo method of budgeting.

An objective examination of the budgeting process within the traditional church context shows that there are some inherent weaknesses in the status quo method. Some of these deficiencies show themselves to be characteristics that work against an effective budgeting process:

- *Budget planning*. A church needs to determine priorities of ministry because there is no other way to measure the effective use of funds (i.e., earning a profit).
- *Revenue budgeting*. Churches have special difficulties in the recognition and budgeting of revenues.
- *Expense budgeting*. In preparing and using expense budgets, churches often find it difficult to match expenses incurred in delivery of services to those revenues that support those services.
- *Measuring effectiveness and control*. Most churches have difficulty measuring effectiveness in meeting budgeted service levels.
- *Budget adaptability*. Church budgets are often difficult to modify once established. From year to year, budget allocations tend to be determined on an incremental basis.
- *Budget participants*. The nonprofit budgeting process involves participants who have widely varying backgrounds and objectives.

- *Church structure.* The church organizational structure often impedes the development of an effective budgeting system.[11]

Projecting cash flow relating to revenue and expenses is fundamental to the church's ability to plan and budget resources. You simply cannot effectively plan a church without planning its finances, which in essence is the purpose of forecasting.

Beyond the Basics

Before we move forward, we need to be sure a few assumptions are firmly in place:

1. The value and justification of a church budget is well accepted.
2. Budgets are a necessary management tool.
3. Furthermore, it should be understood that budgets are more than a control mechanism. They provide an invaluable device for measuring goals while monitoring for a minimum of overexpenditure and waste.

The next step beyond the basics of budgeting has to do with the refining process. The majority of churches in America use a straight-line, twelve-month budget model. (See Exhibit 7–3.) This is practical only if income and expenses are predictable from year to year. Churches experiencing a small amount of steady growth can accommodate a straight-line, or fixed, budget. However, churches with rapid growth, various start-up ministries, and volatile external "X" factors might consider a flexible budget or even the modified zero-based budget approach.

The Fixed Budget

This is the most common church budget. In government or large nonprofit organizations, it is sometimes referred to as an appropriation budget. Generally speaking, it is established for a definite period of time in advance and is not subject to change or alteration during the budget period (unless the leadership of the church decides to offer supplementary changes).

The fixed budget is useful when the church leaders are reasonably certain that conditions of income and expense will remain constant. No significant deviations from the forecast are expected. In this case, the additional time and expense of developing alternative or more refined budgets is unnecessary.

The fixed or traditional budget is based on a single best estimate of income and costs. A figure is determined that represents income for a total year. This amount, along with last year's expenditure total, is then divided by twelve. The result is an annual twelve-month budget in twelve equal periods.

11. Adapted from H. W. Sweeny and Robert Rachlin, *Handbook of Budgeting* (New York: John Wiley, 1981).

The Flexible Budget

The flexible budget, in contrast, is especially suited for those churches in which operating costs are variable at different time periods or levels of activity. As a manager, you need to know that a flexible budget will require more of your time in the forecasting and monitoring phases.

Additionally, a flexible budget means that managers need to be aware of line-item costs. The advantage, though, is that it permits all individual cost items to be "flexed" and altered to accommodate variations.

The advantages of flexible budgeting far outweigh the drawbacks:

- *Ability to update.* Church leadership and department heads are not required to work with an outdated or unrealistic budget. Sudden economic shifts, resulting in many of the aspects mentioned in the section on forecasting, can occur. Under these circumstances, fixed budgets can become difficult to work with and in some cases are useless.
- *Provides for opportunities.* Fixed budgets prevent the church from taking full advantage of opportunities that suddenly arise. New ministry opportunities are often met with resistance and the age-old reminder "It's not in the budget!" Flexible budgets permit leadership to adapt to and even capitalize on these open doors.
- *Realistic guidelines.* With a flexible budget, the increase and decrease of income and expenses are the control mechanisms used for decision making, not the fixed budget that was established perhaps months ago. A flexible budget allows the church leadership the freedom to change directions as circumstances dictate.

For our purposes, we will examine two common varieties of the flexible budget concept.

1. Simple-Average Flexible Budget

In this type of budget model, the same three estimates of income and costs are developed and then averaged. For example, giving for the month of February based on past estimates could realistically be one of three figures: $100,000, $110,000, or $115,000. These three projections would then be charted, with the average being $108,000. (See Exhibit 7–4.)

The main disadvantage to this method is that the financial manager is assigning an equal weight to each of the projections. It is three separate but equal scenarios. Although this is unlikely, the simple-average flexible budget is the simplest to prepare and present for approval. That is because the preparation time is shorter. Also, it is less complicated and therefore easier to understand and present for approval.

Although this type of budget shows a projection for revenue, it naturally follows that the same variations in income also follow for the expense side. If contributions are expected to rise and fall, then expenses should also be budgeted to coincide with the income stream. Otherwise, if giving drops and there are no cash reserves, the church may have to turn to one or both of two options: securing a line of credit at a local bank or curtailing expenses further.

2. Weighted-Average Flexible Budget

In the weighted-average flexible budget, managers can go one step further and even assign a certain level of probability to each of the three projections. Obviously, this requires more research into past income patterns and a tighter internal accounting system.

The advantage, however, is that three separate, distinct projections are prepared. This in turn presents church leaders with options. The traditional method of budgeting usually results in belt-tightening when income drops. Often those reductions are across-the-board, which in many cases is either unfair or unjustified. Exhibit 7–5 is intended to illustrate how the figures for this budget type can be assembled in an understandable fashion.

These two types of flexible budgets are useful in different environments. The decision of which one to adopt depends on the complexity of the ministry, the sophistication of the accounting department, and the importance of the budget to overall church goals.

The Zero-Based Budget

It has been well-established that once a church sets its goals for a specific period of time (usually a year), a budget then becomes an extension of that planning process. Finances become an indispensable resource in carrying out those goals.

However, where many churches have problems is in determining what is the best course of action when revenue begins to drop. The call usually goes out, "Cut the budget!" Often a reduction in spending is in line with the present demand to reduce expenses, but which expenses should the church cut? Which activities should be curtailed? Which employees need to have their hours cut back or even be laid off?

Most churches, when faced with this dilemma, try to be fair and equitable. That is because church boards and congregations, by and large, are governed by a majority rule standard, which, when translated, means a great deal of "give and take." The result is often a vote to either cut what is considered "fat" or mandate an across-the-board reduction of expenses. This usually takes the form of a percentage cut in spending.

The major flaw in this approach is that it doesn't take into consideration the issue of the church's objectives or goals. That is to say, there needs to be an honest evaluation of specific departments and their contribution to the overall goals of the church. Unfortunately, in an effort to be fair, everyone suffers, or (as is the case with those ministries that are essential) some don't suffer but benefit. The benefit comes from the fact that they are considered important enough to be maintained right along with the mis-

114

sionaries, senior pastor's salary, and the utilities. Can every program or expense have equal importance and impact on the overall direction and goals of the church?

Zero-based budgeting (ZBB) avoids many of the common problems associated with the traditional budgeting approach. It permits an evaluation of current operations. Furthermore, it reduces the protection of a ministry simply because it exists, despite the fact that it may not be necessary. ZBB also eliminates across-the-board budget cuts. Finally, it allows participation in the budgeting process by all department heads.

Since our discussion deals with churches, we will move away from the standard zero-based approach used by profit-oriented organizations. Instead, we will modify the ZBB concept to conform to the local church environment. However, the basic justification and principles behind this budgeting method remain the same; we will simply adapt them to the church environment.

Who's on First?

The first step in the zero-based budget process is for the board to determine which areas of the ministry are considered essential. In this prioritizing or ranking process, general overhead requirements need to be included.

For instance, if the church has a mortgage, the board cannot consider the debt as less important than funding a children's sports program. The reason is obvious: if it comes to cost cutting, you cannot set aside the mortgage in favor of the sports activities. Certain areas simply take priority even though they are not considered "pure ministry." The same would hold true with utilities, insurance, taxes, and what would be considered fixed expenses.

Therefore, in the process of placing priorities, the board needs to include those fixed expense areas as "packages" right along with a package of support for missions, youth, and other ministries.

What's in the Package?

To begin, packages or decision units need to be determined based on the priorities of the church. Package number one, due to its obvious importance, would be what business managers consider fixed expenses. They are mortgage/rent, utilities, taxes, insurance, basic phone service, and any other overhead item that is required to keep the church doors open.

Package number two would contain the basic compensation package of the senior pastor. Let's be honest here—without him in the pulpit each week, more than likely your offerings would drop. He is essential to the viability of the church.

But in certain cases, there may be some who say, "No, it is the strong music program or the youth ministry that brings the people into the church." If that is the case, then the basic funding of that ministry moves to the second position.

Do you see what is happening here? The church is being broken down into operating units and then arranged by priority based on their contribution to the overall requirements and goals of the church. That is why basic costs are stressed instead of a single expense unit. That is, the phone bill is reduced to its lowest operational level in package number one. The pastor's compensation is reduced to salary and insurance but not added perks. We are after the lowest denominator in dealing with expenses.

Package number three may contain further administrative overhead items or a particular ministry area. Again, at the lower zero-based levels, we stick with the basics of the ministry with no frills or extras.

On it goes until you have all your annual projected budget broken down into packages and by priority.

Simply stated, the package should contain the following information:

✔ Who is the preparer, and what is the date of preparation?
✔ What is the purpose and description of activity or ministry?
✔ What is its cost, and what is the nature of all required resources?
✔ What are the expected benefits and results?
✔ What are the consequences if the activity is not funded?
✔ What is the recommended level at which the package should be funded?

Perhaps you have noticed by now that participation by your department heads or lay leaders involved in that ministry package is essential. If one person creates all the packages, you will not have one of the major budgeting principles in place—participation. If the budget is prepared "from on high" and set in place, the people operating within the framework of the budget will not be as committed to its success as they would be if they had a part in developing it. They would not "own" the budget and, therefore, would not have bought into the process of seeing that it works. (For sample budget package charts and worksheet, see Exhibits 7–6, 7–7, and 7–8.)

Ranking the Packages

Ultimately, some authoritative group will have to rank the packages by their priority. As unpopular as this may sound on the surface, down the road it will eliminate a lot of problems. It may be the Budget Committee who decides and then presents it to the church board. Depending on your church polity, it may end there, or it may be presented to the congregation for approval.

The primary issue is that you will be spending money as it becomes available on a monthly basis. If more money is available, then packages with lower priorities can be funded.

A question to consider at this point is, What if you just want to partially fund a program? Let's use the missions program as an example. Using this method of budgeting, missions can still receive a high priority. The important projects can receive money while the less crucial will be placed on the "back burner." Their budgets are tiered or divided into essential and less essential activities.

No doubt, the first two or three packages will be absolutely vital, with no anticipated cuts. However, it is advisable to divide the other ministries into sections, separating out the important from the "wish list" category. Thus, you have what could be called a modified zero-based budget.

True ZBB takes every cost, starts at a zero base and builds from that point. That may be a little too extreme for most churches because of their somewhat democratic way of making decisions. Much of what is decided in a church requires consensus, and the pure zero-based approach may not be that easy to explain or accept. It says that one ministry is more important than another.

However, by modifying the ZBB concept as I have described, you can actually fund *all* the ministries. It is the level *within* the ministries that can be adjusted.

Packages, therefore, are normally placed into three categories:

1. *Nondiscretionary and legally required packages.* This group would more than likely be fully funded.

2. *Discretionary packages.* This is always the largest group, and some of the ministries might have to be ranked. However, it is possible to place all current or essential ministries in this category. It needs to be understood though that there may be a time when the funds could run out, and certain projects within these packages will not be funded. Therefore, the items in the package need to be ranked to ensure money for the important items, followed by the less essential. (Again, do you see the importance of having the department heads involved in the budgeting process?)

3. *Wish-list packages.* This third group doesn't necessarily need to be ranked unless it is rather certain one or two of them will be funded, especially if it is necessary to make reductions later in the fiscal year. With the zero-based concept in place, it allows everyone to know what is going to happen because of the priority setting and ranking.

Summary

A successful zero-based program will increase the participation of all department heads in the budgeting process. This often encourages cost effectiveness, sometimes eliminates inefficiencies, and permits a great deal of flexibility in decision making. Church leaders are not tied down to a set annual budget with line-items firmly voted in place.

However, you need to know that zero-based budgeting demands more time and energy than conventional budgeting. Everyone involved will be forced to abandon traditional budgeting practices and accept an entirely different approach to resource allocation.

If you believe that the zero-based concept is too drastic a change, you could adopt it the first year by assigning only a few packages. That is, use the conventional, straight-line, twelve-month budget, but set the funding level slightly lower than full capacity. Then establish two or three packages at the wish-list level. If funds are available, then money can be directed to these areas. It is possible to establish the ZBB program over a period of two or three years using this phase-in approach.

Zero-based budgeting is designed to make maximum use of the church's resources. Conventional budgeting, while easier to explain to the congregation and certainly simpler to administer, still assumes that previous budgets were valid and, therefore, a correct base to build upon.

A zero-based budget, on the other hand, says that each year the funding base begins at zero. Department heads and supervisors look at their own activities and say, "This is what I want to do, and this is how much it will cost." ZBB requires managers to also work from the ground up.

Keeping Your Finger on the Pulse

The annual budget should be reviewed on a regular, periodic basis. Usually, a monthly report of income and expense is used. Some ministries expand this information to show both a combined and individual department report. This combined statement depicts all the totals for a certain line-item. (See Exhibit 7–9.)

The departmental budget report shows income and expenses by department and by line-item. (See Exhibit 7–10.)

The accepted practice when preparing a more formalized report is to express the reporting periods as *Current* (the present accounting period) and *Year to Date* (activity for the months elapsed in the fiscal year). Most computerized accounting packages provide this information in their general ledger modules under a monthly income statement.

On a quarterly basis, it is a good practice to measure revenue against expenses. (See Exhibit 7–11.) Simply determine a quarter's income versus expenses, with a variance (difference) comparison. Some managers like to see the dollar or percentage of income remaining in the unexpended portion of the budget.

Finally, at the end of the fiscal year, a summarized report of revenue and expense should be prepared. (See Exhibit 7–12.) This report ideally should be broken out by quarters. To simplify matters, a summary report of the budget line-items could be presented instead of a full report of all line-items. A more detailed report could be available for those who need this information. However, leaders on the church board would no doubt be satisfied with a simple summary report.

Conclusion

The advantage of an accurate, thorough budget is effective planning, coordination, and control. The primary advantage of budgeting is that it forces managers to evaluate and think qualitatively about the overall ministry of the church, its strengths and weaknesses, and where it is headed or where it should be headed. By its very nature, budgeting requires leadership to identify problems and their possible solutions early in the budgeting process.

The process of budgeting mandates periodic review and revision of basic policies for the entire organization. The budget is often the single common thread weaving through the entire structure and ministry of the church.

Coordination of effort within the organizational structure is perhaps the primary reason most churches need a budget, whether leaders know it or not. Only when the actions of all the ministry departments are properly synchronized can an organization function efficiently.

Budgets are also a tool to help ensure that church resources are directed to the areas where they are needed. Optimum efficiency and balance of all aspects of a church are seldom possible. After all, it is essentially an "all-volunteer army." However, a carefully prepared budget will certainly minimize inefficiency and imbalance.

Once a current and meaningful budget is established, succeeding budgets will benefit by anticipating potential trouble spots and providing a framework for early solution.

The true success of a budget cannot and should not be measured by how close it comes to actual performance. A budget can also be effective by emphasizing the differences of projections from actual performance and by permitting critical analysis and study of those differences.

Exhibit 7–1
Three-Year Analysis of Past Giving Patterns

"Looking back" means a simple analysis of past giving patterns. Below is an example of a graph depeciting giving over a three-year period.

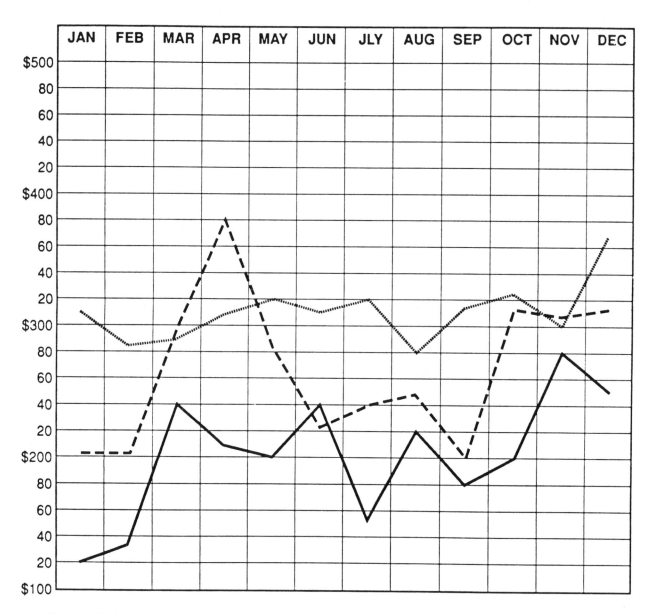

The analysis should show seasonal variations and other special fluctuations. The differences should be identified and understood.

1988 ———————— 1989 — — — — — — 1990 ·····················

Exhibit 7–2
Cash-Flow Graph

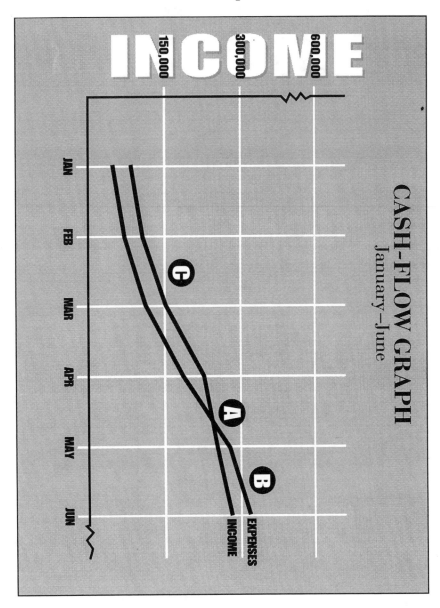

Exhibit 7–3
Straight-Line Budget

STRAIGHT LINE BUDGET

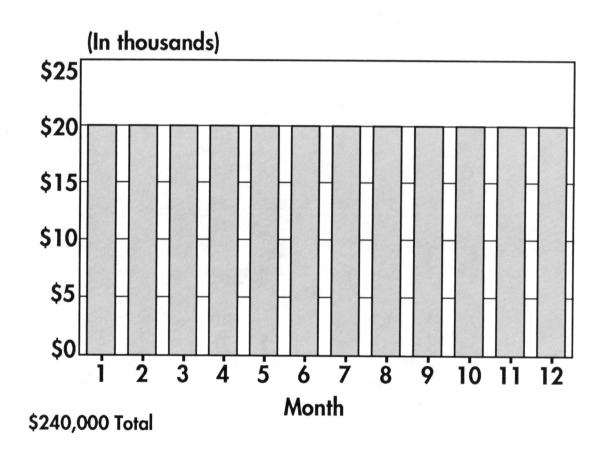

(In thousands)

$240,000 Total

Exhibit 7–4
Averaged Budget

AVERAGED BUDGET

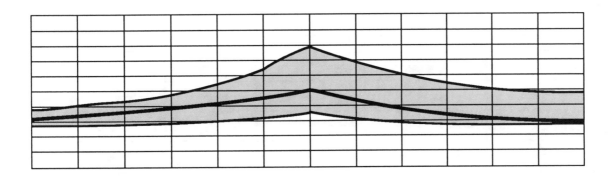

Exhibit 7–5
Unaveraged Budget

UNAVERAGED BUDGET

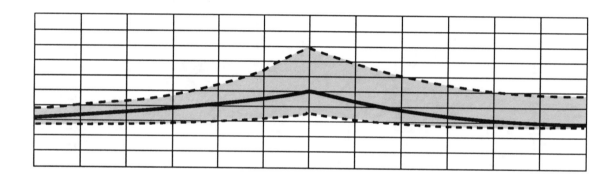

Exhibit 7–6
Sample Funding

SAMPLE FUNDING

Zero Based Budget Packages
Allocation of Church Funds

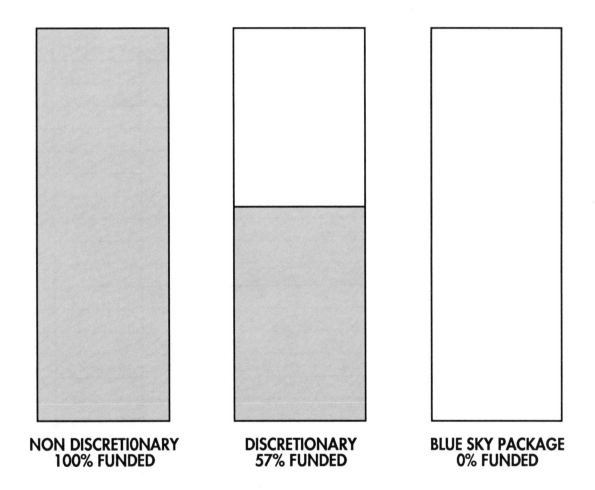

NON DISCRETIONARY
100% FUNDED

DISCRETIONARY
57% FUNDED

BLUE SKY PACKAGE
0% FUNDED

Exhibit 7–7
Budget Package Form

BUDGET PACKAGE

Fiscal Year 19___

Ministry/Activity: _____

Name of Preparer: _____

Date: _____

Key to Ranking: **A** = Nondiscretionary
B = Discretionary
C = Optional (wish list)

G/L #	Description	$ Amount	Ranking

Page ___ of ___

Exhibit 7–8
Budget Package Sample

BUDGET PACKAGE

Fiscal Year 19___

Ministry/Activity: _____

Name of Preparer: _____

Date: _____

Key to Ranking: **A** = Nondiscretionary
B = Discretionary
C = Optional (wish list)

G/L #	Description	$ Amount	Ranking
7010:0070	Salaries	To Be Determined	
7810:0070	Benefits	To Be Determined	
8410:0070	Supplies - Office	$200	B
8020:0070	Promotional Materials	$500	B
8372:0070	Non-Capital Equipment	$2000	C
8375:0070	Lease-Rental	$1500	B
8245:0070	Supplies - Music	$1000	A
8481:0070	Printing - Internal	$750	A/B
8480:0070	Printing - External	$750	B
8430:0070	Postage	$350	A
8374:0070	Maintenance - Equipment	$500	A
8400:0070	Supplies - Data Processing	$200	B
8420:0070	Books, Tapes, Subscriptions	$300	C
8645:0070	Purchased Services	$800	B
8665:0070	Special Activities	$500	B
8680:0070	Christmas Concert	$2200	A
8675:0070	Easter Concert (Special Music)	$2500	A
8670:0070	Retreats	$500	C
8690:0070	Food Service	$300	B
8660:0070	Seminars/Conferences	$500	B
8650:0070	Multimedia	$400	B

Exhibit 7–9
Summary of Expenses Examples

Summary of Expenses

	Current	Budget	$ Variance	% Var	Year-To-Date	Budget	$ Variance	% Var
Income								
Tithes and Offerings								
Tithes and Offerings	$113,090	$118,035	($5,745)	(4.83)	$744,268	$713,012	$31,256	4.38
Catch Up Offering	0	0	0	0.00	0	0	0	0.00
Building Fund Offerings	40,315	56,667	(16,352)	(28.86)	250,089	340,000	(89,911)	(26.44)
Missions Project Offering	4,760	3,333	1,427	42.81	12,194	20,000	(7,806)	(39.03)
Deacons Fund Offering	462	833	(371)	(44.54)	4,898	5,000	(102)	(2.04)
Mission Project Sunday	0	0	0	0.00	0	0	0	0.00
Organ Fund	90	0	90	0.00	720	0	720	0.00
Teresa Memorial	0	0	0	0.00	0	0	0	0.00
Love Offerings	0	0	0	0.00	511	0	511	0.00
Misc. Dept. Offerings	0	0	0	0.00	0	0	0	0.00
Total Tithes & Offerings	158,717	179,668	(20 951)	(11.66)	1,012,680	1,078,012	(65,332)	(6.06)
Other Income								
Tape Ministry	331	0	331	0.00	1,575	0	1,575	0.00
Video Ministry	0	0	0	0.00	2,000	0	2,000	0.00
Daily Bread	45	0	45	0.00	41	0	41	0.00
Special Music Programs	0	0	0	0.00	(2,810)	0	(2,810)	(0.00)
Wedding Income	610	0	610	0.00	2,320	0	2,320	0.00
~~								
Awana Income	0	0	0	0.00	0	0	0	0.00
Total Other Income	10,834	4,340	6,494	149.63	85,012	26,048	58,964	226.37
Total Income	169,551	184,008	(14,457)	(7.86)	1,097,692	1,104,060	(6,368)	(0.58)
Transfer of Funds								
Deacon Fund Transfers	1,214	0	1,214	0.00	5,489	0	5,489	0.00
Love Offering Transfer	0	0	0	0.00	0	0	0	0.00
Miscellaneous Inc. Trns.	0	0	0	0.00	0	0	0	0.00
Total Transfer of Funds	1,214	0	1,214	0.00	5,489	0	5,489	0.00
General & Admin. Costs								
Cash (Over/Short)	0	0	0	0.00	0	0	0	0.00
Salaries	35,138	25,796	9,342	36.21	142,419	154,772	(12,353)	(7.98)
Non-Employee Compens.	20,505	14,937	5,568	37.28	86,104	89,618	(3,514)	(3.92)
Housing Allowance	19,807	14,249	5,558	39.01	78,278	85,496	(7,218)	(8.44)
~~								
Interest Income	0	0	0	0.00	0	0	0	0.00
Gain/Loss Sale Assets	0	0	0	0.00	0	0	0	0.00
Project Development	675	0	675	0.00	0	0	29,512	0.00
Amort. Exp. Bond Iss. Cost	0	0	0	0.00	0	0	0	0.00
Total G & A Costs	189,079	170,538	18,541	10.87	918,191	1,013,971	(95,780)	(9.45)
Net Income or Loss	($20,742)	$13,470	($34,212)	(253.99)	$174,012	$90,089	$83,923	93.16

128

Exhibit 7–10
Summary of Expenses Examples

First Church
Departmental Statement of Operations
0054 - Jr. High School
Budget vs. Actual
for the six months ended June 30, 19___

	Current	Budget	$ Variance	% Var	Year-To-Date	Budget	$ Variance	% Var
Income								
Tithes and Offerings								
Missions Project Offering	$0	$0	$0	0.00	$0	$0	$0	0.00
Total Tithes & Offerings	0	0	0	0.00	0	0	0	0.00
Other Income								
Seminars & Conferences	0	0	0	0.00	0	0	0	0.00
Camps & Retreats	2,093	833	1,260	151.26	3,985	5,000	(1,015)	(20.30)
Special Activities	0	0	0	0.00	0	0	0	0.00
Missions Projects	12	0	12	0.00	52	0	52	0.00
Total Other Income	2,105	833	1,272	152.70	4,037	5,000	(963)	(19.26)
Total Income	2,105	833	1,272	152.70	4,037	5,000	(963)	(19.36)
Transfer of Funds								
Total Transfer of Funds	0	0	0	0.00	0	0	0	0.00
General & Admin. Costs								
Salaries	1,458	1,000	458	45.80	4,896	6,000	(1,104)	(18.40)
Non-Employee Compens.	137	92	45	48.91	549	553	(4)	(0.72)
Housing Allowance	375	249	126	50.60	1,500	1,496	4	0.27
Honorarium Travel & Exp.	0	21	(21)	(100.00)	0	124	(124)	(100.00)
Hon.-Speaking, Music, Other	0	0	0	0.00	0	0	0	0.00
Vacation Accural Adjmt.	0	0	0	0.00	0	0	0	0.00
FICA Tax Expense	94	0	94	0.00	352	0	352	0.00
Workers Compensation	0	20	(20)	(100.00)	0	120	(120)	(100.00)
Health Insurance	56	0	56	0.00	145	0	145	0.00
Life Insurance	0	16	(16)	(100.00)	25	98	(73)	(74.49)
Retirement Costs	0	0	0	0.00	0	0	0	0.00
Lease & Rental - Vehicle	0	0	0	0.00	0	0	0	0.00
Vehicle Cgs. Internal	0	0	0	0.00	0	0	0	0.00
Seminars & Conferences	0	13	(13)	(100.00)	0	75	(75)	(100.00)
Special Activities	0	50	(50)	(100.00)	0	300	(300)	(100.00)
Missions Project	42	8	34	425.00	84	52	32	61.54
Camps & Retreat	2,221	167	2,054	----.---	5,651	1,000	4,651	465.10
Food Service	0	0	0	0.00	0	0	0	0.00
Total G & A Costs	4,496	1,882	2,614	138.89	14,048	11,302	2,746	24.30
Net Income or Loss	($2,391)	($1,049)	($1,342)	(127.93)	($10,011)	($6,302)	($3,709)	(58.85)

129

Exhibit 7–11
Quarterly Budget Report Sample

FIRST CHURCH

Quarterly Budget Report

Three months ended March 31, 19___

	First Quarter Budget	First Quarter Actual	Variance Favorable (Unfavorable)	Unexpended Budget
REVENUE				
General Offerings	220,000	225,000	(5,000)	655,000
Building Fund	85,000	82,000	3,000	249,000
Missions Offerings	7,000	6,800	200	19,200
Special Projects	0	0	0	8,000
Misc. Income	1,000	1,200	(200)	11,800
TOTAL REVENUE	$313,000	$315,000	($2,000)	$943,000
EXPENSES				
Personnel Costs	147,900	147,500	400	444,100
Missions	15,000	14,550	450	45,450
General & Admin.	55,000	57,000	(2,000)	163,000
Building Expenses	82,000	83,000	(1,000)	245,000
TOTAL EXPENSE	$299,900	$302,050	($2,150)	$897,550

Exhibit 7–12
Annual Revenue & Expense Budget Sample

FIRST CHURCH

Revenue & Expense Budget FY 19___

	First Quarter	Second Quarter	Third Quarter	Fourth Quarter	Totals
REVENUES					
General Offerings	220,000	225,000	190,000	245,000	880,000
Building Fund	85,000	90,000	60,000	96,000	331,000
Missions Offering	7,000	6,000	5,900	8,000	26,900
Special Projects	0	5,000	0	3,000	8,000
Misc. Income	1,000	1,000	10,000	1,000	13,000
	....	....	....	....	....
TOTAL REVENUES	313,000	327,000	265,900	353,000	1,258,900
	::::::::::::	::::::::::::	::::::::::::	::::::::::::	::::::::::::
EXPENSES					
Salaries	112,000	112,000	120,000	120,000	464,000
Benefits	20,500	20,000	20,500	20,500	82,000
Payroll Taxes	11,000	11,000	11,800	11,800	45,600
Missions Support	7,000	7,000	7,000	7,000	28,000
Honorariums	3,000	2,500	3,500	3,000	12,000
Utilities	6,000	4,500	7,000	4,000	21,500
Telephone	3,300	3,300	3,300	3,300	13,200
Promo/Advertising	1,500	1,500	1,500	1,500	6,000
Repairs/Maintenance	1,200	1,300	1,100	1,100	4,700
Curriculum/Books	1,200	200	3,000	500	4,900
Graphics/Printing	2,000	2,000	2,000	2,000	8,000
Maint. Contracts	3,000	3,000	3,000	3,000	12,000
Music Supplies	5,000	5,500	4,000	5,200	19,700
Office Supplies	625	625	625	625	2,500
Janitorial Supplies	675	675	675	675	2m700
Data Processing	2,000	2,000	2,000	2,000	8,000
Insurance	3,500	3,500	3,500	3,500	14,000
Depreciation	3,250	3,250	3,250	3,250	13,000
Travel/Entertain.	1,000	1,500	1,300	1,800	5,600
Mileage	3,000	3,000	2,000	3,500	11,500
Missions Projects	0	5,000	0	5,000	10,000
Camps/Retreats	2,000	1,500	10,000	1,500	15,000
Building Expenses	95,000	93,000	80,000	60,000	328,000
Professional Services	1,000	1,000	1,000	1,000	4,000
Food Service	3,600	4,000	2,500	5,000	15,100
Misc. Expense	5,000	5,000	5,000	5,000	20,000
	....	....	....	....	....
TOTAL EXPENSE	297,350	298,350	299,550	275,750	1,171,000
	::::::::::::	::::::::::::	::::::::::::	::::::::::::	::::::::::::

Chapter 8

Obstacles to Good Stewardship

C ertain hindrances to good stewardship and effective management of church financial resources are often present at the local church level. These barriers are not always readily recognized, yet their effect is strong.

The Challenge of a Clear Vision

Without a doubt, overly ambitious building programs have caused more stress in churches than any other financial endeavor. After seeing the price tag for some of these buildings, you begin to wonder if the original purpose of the project justifies the cost. Many building programs have pursued what has been termed "architectural evangelism." The motto taken from the movie *Field of Dreams* is "Build it and they will come!" It is felt that a large, ornate sanctuary will draw people to the church. But will they come to Christ because of the seating capacity?

A primary obstacle to good stewardship is sometimes no more than a lack of good old-fashioned common sense. Of course, there are many instances where growth demands a larger facility. But at what cost? Unfortunately, some church boards get carried away when it comes to planning building programs. It could be compared to the marketing department of a company designing the new corporate headquarters—a lot of form but very little content!

Almost everyone agrees that the local church consists of more than simply bricks and mortar. But, then again, almost every church spends a great deal of time, energy, and money on buildings. It is interesting to note that the greatest emphasis is on the building, ambience, and sound system when leaders speak of a setting for a worship service. Jerry White has written, "The emphasis on a sanctuary, 'coming into the presence of God,' or even quietness in the meeting room all focus on the building as a sacred place rather than a functional tool for the ministry of the local church."[12]

Over the years I have been asked dozens of times how an expanding church congregation can get into a larger facility. People have called me to ask how to build a church and somehow avoid the pitfalls and cash-flow problems of heavy borrowing.

I am pleased to report that there are countless churches across America that are both large and thriving who have chosen to avoid debt. They have decided to build debt free and, in some cases, have delayed expanding until they could afford to do so. The "sanctuaries" of many of these congregations range from rented storefronts, schools, and vacated grocery stores to converted warehouses. I am aware of two churches in Southern California—one rents a high school on Sunday with an attendance of about 4,000, and the other has converted a warehouse into a 1,200-seat auditorium that even has a balcony.

It goes without saying that most of these congregations are meeting in what even they admit are makeshift facilities, but how do you account for their growth if you have to have your own building to be a growing congregation? Most of these folks would tell you they'd like to "own their own place," but, since they're committed to avoiding debt, they are relying on effective programming and solid teaching. At this point, the church is in their hearts, not in a building.

I realize that my opinions are not shared by most church leaders today. The building-for-God mentality is alive and well. It is assumed that God prefers to be worshiped in great edifices of glass and steel. I believe the mistake is that sometimes these buildings are monuments to an architect and may draw the curious to an engineering marvel, but does it draw people to Christ? Or is this a further extension of the "me" generation? After all, "I deserve to attend the best-looking church in town." We drive good-looking cars, live in good-looking houses, wear good-looking clothes; why not attend a good-looking church and complete the total look?

The argument can also be made that this is "the Lord's house." Just look at the beauty and workmanship of the Old Testament temple in Jerusalem, which God Himself designed! But the tabernacle and the temple no longer exist. In His discussion with the Samaritan woman at the well, Christ said that true worship is "in spirit and truth" (John 4:23). Paul went further when he said that even if our very own bodies were to perish, "we have a building from God, a house not made with hands" (2 Corinthians 5:1). To place this entire issue into a proper perspective, I believe that two essential questions need to be answered before spending church resources on buildings.

First, what is the true motive for building or expansion? Is it based on a real or perceived need? Are you actually out of Sunday school space, or would you just like to have a nicer facility? In my mind, there is nothing wrong with wanting more space, a

---

12. Jerry White, *The Church and the Parachurch* (Portland, Ore.: Multnomah, 1983), 42.

more modern, efficient building, or added facilities. The issue here is motive: Are we doing this to compete with other churches? Is this money going to be spent to the detriment of missions or essential programs?

One of the most dangerous arguments for financially overextending a congregation is the mind-set "If we don't take care of Jerusalem first, we won't be able to send money to Judea and the 'uttermost parts' of the earth." Translated, if we neglect the home church, money won't flow in and therefore funds won't be available for outreach programs. Unfortunately, it is entirely possible that the root of this attitude is the looking-out-for-number-one sentiment. The Great Commission never said anything about highly leveraged building programs.

The second question is one of a very practical nature. *What effect will borrowing have on the cash flow of the church?* It is not unusual for large churches to endure $40,000- to $80,000-a-month mortgage payments. Consequently, during the last recession, the default rate on church bonds and mortgages increased dramatically. In my role as a church administrative consultant, I have counseled many churches as they struggled with these heavy debt loads. In nearly every instance, it required substantial cuts in programs and ministry spending in order to service the loans. I have told church leaders many times that a large debt-to-income ratio produces an "800-pound gorilla." Each week, the gorilla sits at the front of your church service. He waits until the offering is taken and then removes his portion first—that is, before you have paid the pastor, the light bill, or the missionaries.

The point is obvious: a large mortgage reorders all the church's priorities. You pay the loan first; everything else comes next. Truly, "the borrower becomes the lender's slave" (Proverbs 22:7).

In the early nineties, a philosophy was being taught that a church should expect a certain amount of debt. In fact, it was referred to as "reasonable debt." The line of reasoning goes something like this: Healthy, growing churches have a reasonable debt of 15 to 30 percent of their budgets; stagnant churches have no debt and no vision to grow; floundering churches have excessive debt of 30 to 50 percent. Floundering churches cannot support effective ministries, and they hurt their growth with constant pleading for money.

The basic flaw in that notion is one of simple mathematics. If, as the growth experts say, 15 to 30 percent is normal, then let's simply run that argument out to the end of the cash-flow equation.

> 30 percent for mortgage payment
> 50 percent for staff compensation, including benefits
> + 10 percent for mission support
> 90 percent

With ninety cents out of every dollar already accounted for, that leaves ten cents for programming, utilities, building maintenance, and so forth. Ten cents to cover the dozens of other line-items associated with running a vibrant local church ministry! Reasonable debt? If this is reasonable and evidence of a healthy, growing church, what would you call all those churches prior to the sixties that didn't borrow heavily? Many of those churches were the foundations for the churches of today, and for the most part they were debt free.

In 1991, an article entitled "The Bible or the Bank?" appeared in a newsletter published by Christian Financial Concepts and written by Larry Burkett. Because this essay addresses this issue so accurately and succinctly, it has been reproduced here, by permission, in its entirety.

The Bible or the Bank?

Church borrowing is an emotional and controversial topic. It is difficult to teach on this subject directly because it is primarily an attitude rather than an issue. However, anything taken to excess is destructive, and certainly that is true of debt.

The use of debt to build or expand the outreach of a church is so common today that even to challenge the idea can create an air of animosity. But just because a practice is "normal" doesn't mean it is scriptural or "best." It should be noted that most churches repay their debts according to a contract. So the discussion is not whether a church can repay . . . they must repay. It is whether or not churches should borrow even if they can repay.

Scriptural Guidelines

Borrowing is not prohibited in Scripture. It is discouraged. But there are no positive references to borrowing, and, in fact, there are explicit warnings to avoid it. "The rich rules over the poor, and the borrower becomes the lender's slave" (Proverbs 22:7). Thus, the Word indicates that an unnecessary authority is created by borrowing.

The question is often asked, "If borrowing is allowable for individuals, why shouldn't churches also be able to borrow?" In the first place, much of the borrowing done by individual Christians is, itself, unscriptural because it is done in excess. This can be witnessed in the current level of divorce and bankruptcy, both of which are primarily motivated by the excessive use of credit.

It is clear that standards for leaders in the church are more stringent than for the individual members (1 Timothy 3:1–2). If this is so (and it is), then it would be obvious that the standards of the church organization must be higher than those of its individual members.

Scriptural Precedent

After looking at borrowing in the Scriptures, I came to several conclusions:

- One, borrowing is always presented in the negative (see Proverbs 17:18).
- Two, God never once made a promise to anyone and then fulfilled it through a loan (see Luke 6:38).
- Three, God promised His people that, if they would obey His commandments, they wouldn't have to borrow (see Deuteronomy 28:12).
- Four, God had worship structures built at least three times in the Bible, and no credit was used.

It might be said that these aren't valid examples because borrowing wasn't a formal practice during these times. If not, then Solomon wasted many proverbs dealing with the dangers of too much credit.

In the New Testament, the attitudes reflected in Acts 4 and 2 Corinthians 8 would indicate a commitment to giving whatever is needed.

Why Not Borrow?

"If money is borrowed by a church to do God's work and is repaid in a timely fashion, what's the harm?" This question is logical and is frequently asked. Here are several answers:

1. Each church leader and member must search God's Word with an open mind and heart to determine if God does or doesn't desire churches to be funded with debt. If it is determined that to borrow is a compromise of God's will, then to do so is sin. "Therefore, to one who knows the right thing to do and does not do it, to him it is sin" (James 4:17).

2. Borrowing denies God's people the opportunity to experience His overwhelming blessings in response to giving what is clearly within His will (2 Corinthians 9:10). We are told in 1 John 3:22 that we can ask of God and expect to receive. Certainly this would be true of the needs of the church. The experience of seeing God provide through His people is a witness to those within and without the church.

3. A debt within the church restricts the ability of the members to serve God. Quite often, ministry decisions are based on the need to meet the debt payments rather than to fund current ministry needs.

4. Often, the ability to repay the debt depends on the ability of the pastor to preach. In many instances, lenders have required a signed contract from the pastor that he would not leave while the debt existed and would maintain an insurance policy to pay off the debt in the event of his death.

5. Huge portions of church collections go to meet interest payments. This money could be used to further God's kingdom rather than Satan's. Some major denominations spend more on interest payments than on foreign missions.

Other Ministries

There certainly can be no distinction between churches borrowing or other ministries borrowing. If an organization holds itself out to be an instrument of Jesus Christ, it should strive to meet God's standard.

Having faced the same choices in a ministry, I find the need to wait upon God's provision in advance to be confining. However, it is also freeing. If God can direct us by providing, then He can also direct by withholding. Some ministries have borrowed to do things God never intended them to do. Others have borrowed to do God's will but have missed one of God's greatest areas of testimony.

Very few nonbelievers could be convinced that there is anything supernatural or miraculous about a loan. Few would deny that there is something at least "unique" about a debt-free ministry.

I trust that this brief survey will not be viewed as any kind of indictment of churches or other ministries, because it is not. The purpose is to show church and ministry leaders, as well as their members, that God can and will provide (through His people) that which is necessary to do His will.

> So Moses issued a command, and a proclamation was circulated throughout the camp, saying, "Let neither man nor woman any longer perform work for the contributions of the sanctuary." Thus the people were restrained from bringing any more. For the material they had was sufficient and more than enough for all the work, to perform it. (Exodus 36:6–7)[13]

Cultural Challenges

The philosophy of the day says you should have it all—now. This mind-set causes serious problems in the local church. Members who are accustomed to making large purchases using personal credit, carry that same belief system and practice into their church. Many local congregations have assumed staggering amounts of debt over the last decade that have resulted in high debt-service payments. Many of these debts cut deeply into ministry resources to the extent that staffing needs and other opportunities have to be set aside in order to pay the mortgage.

Many families in the church have gotten into serious problems by financing their homes with adjustable mortgages. When mortgage rates increase, their disposable in-

---

13. Used by permission of Larry Burkett, "The Bible or the Bank?" *Christian Financial Concepts*, Gainesville, Ga.

come decreases, and the result is less giving to the church. That isn't the way it is supposed to be, but that's the way it is. Unfortunately, the same holds true for the church's methods of financing building projects, capital improvements, or sometimes even outreach programs. Shouldn't the church be the role model for sound, prudent financial principles?

Edward J. Hales writes, "Sacrificial giving, or even giving on a regular basis, is too often unacceptable to us. Our comfort-driven society and our selfish natures do not readily make room for such Biblical values as 'you gain by losing.' "[14]

In the final analysis, then, church leaders need to be honest with themselves and the congregation. They should ask the tough question "Are we in fact part of the problem?"

The Teaching Challenge

Teaching on the subject of giving, unfortunately, is often laced with negatives, guilt, or exploitation. Frequently, the manner in which this theme is handled is based on where the leadership of the church stands theologically and what is the actual cash-flow situation. Coming from their own theological standpoint, some pastors will restrain themselves when faced with dwindling funds. Their approach is based on one of two beliefs: a notion that more faith in God is needed or the view that talking about money from the pulpit isn't "spiritual."

There are those, however, who see a reduction in cash flow as a signal to address the issue firmly, candidly, and explicitly. From there it can go either in a positive, uplifting direction or in a heavy, crisis-laden direction.

Too often, supporting the Lord's work is viewed as an obligation (sort of like paying your bills) instead of being depicted as a privilege. Paul encourages believers to give with a cheerful heart.

One of the obstacles to effective fund-raising in churches is the challenge of good teaching in this area. Many churches don't know quite what to do about the need to pass the collection plate. Some, in order to appear spiritual or unaffected by such mundane or temporal matters, simply put a box at the back of the church for whomever wishes to make a contribution. There isn't anything inherently wrong with that approach as long as the motives are proper. However, at the risk of sounding facetious, I have seen those "Agape Boxes" gradually move to a more prominent place in the service when the church falls short of its financial goals or commitments. This laid-back style soon (but not always) gives way to the more traditional mode. They too have discovered that "Happiness is positive cash flow!"

14. Edward J. Hales, "The Role of Stewardship in the Local Church," in *Money for Ministries*, ed. Wesley K. Wilmer (Wheaton, Ill.: Victor, 1989), 100.

Numerous churches, in an effort to avoid offending nonchurched "seekers," make every attempt to downplay receiving an offering. They move the offertory to a less prominent place in the the service, apologize to visitors, and ask them to ignore the plate as it goes by. The idea here is to be "seeker friendly" or to avoid disturbing the mood or flow of the worship experience.

Although the Old Testament sets as a minimum standard 10 percent of a person's annual income, studies have shown that most Christians give less than this minimum guideline. An article in *Christianity Today* stated, "On the average, per capita giving was 3.05 percent of disposable income in 1968, but had dropped to 2.79 percent in 1985. From 1985 to 1989, the decline accelerated, dropping even more sharply, by 23%."[15] In other words, giving to churches as a percentage of income declined at a faster rate annually between 1985 and 1989 than it had in previous years. This period was part of the economic boom in our country—prior to the recession of the early nineties. Companies fueled their rapid expansion through leveraging, and church leaders merely copied this philosophy.

The article points out another disturbing trend. "Churches continue to spend a smaller portion of their members' giving on work outside their own needs (benevolence spending) than on work within the congregation."[16] I believe the reason this is taking place is that churches are spending money on building programs and larger staffs. The same vigorous economic activity that secular corporations were experiencing was also taking place in many churches. The boom inevitably resulted in downsizing both corporate America and churches.

Church leaders should realize that it isn't necessary to camouflage the need for funds. Everyone knows that a church needs money to operate. Most civic organizations make no excuses for both their need for money and their requirement to ask for it. In fact, they are usually quite creative in the methods they use in dealing with this economic fact of life. Surely church leaders should not feel apologetic about asking for money on Sunday. The need for donations should be presented as a part of the overall program of the church and not relegated exclusively to that time-honored day called "Stewardship Sunday" or some other annual special emphasis.

I am not suggesting that the theme of giving be a major, dominant part of the life of the church. There should be a balance between teaching and the presentation of needs that portrays giving as a normal part of the flow of worship. It isn't something we ought to feel guilty about; nor should we be overly concerned that we might offend guests. Once again, it all depends on the biblical perspective of raising funds and how it is presented from the pulpit.

15. "Church Giving Continues to Decline," *Christianity Today,* 11 November 1991.
16. Ibid.

The Methodology Challenges

Recent research and articles dealing with the characteristics of today's "baby boomers" indicate that we can no longer count on loyalty when it comes to giving to the church. Major corporations spend millions of dollars to maintain brand loyalty among customers—often to no avail. Edward Hales has said, "In today's world, people need clear teaching and mechanisms for giving that fit where they are in life. Whether the mechanism is providing offering envelopes or estate planning, our methodology must match the different passages people will go through in a lifetime."[17]

Although the issue of the means and the mode of receiving funds into the local church has already been discussed, it must be reemphasized that the method is of paramount importance. Once again, the requirement of a basic philosophy moves to center stage. As soon as the principles are understood and embraced, decisions regarding church finances in general and fund-raising in particular can be addressed. A solid grasp of biblical teaching in this area will go a long way toward eliminating problems as they arise.

For instance, the question of alternate forms of fund-raising come up frequently in churches. Youth groups in particular employ money-making methods other than the collection plate when raising funds. They may have a special project in mind that is not funded through the normal budgetary process, and, for whatever reasons, they feel they need to raise money quickly and without having to go through what may be a lengthy approval process. This is normal and understandable. The scenario usually follows that a request for approval of a fund-raising event comes to the finance committee or its equivalent. The question that needs to be asked then is, "What is our policy regarding car washes, bake sales, walkathons, and raffles? Do we even have a policy?" The leadership is confronted with a request that doesn't fit the mold. Or does it?

Does a high school car wash turn the church property into a "house of merchandise"? Not really. If the church budget is funded primarily through tithes and offerings, then I see nothing wrong with these types of events as long as they are used to pay for non-budgeted expenses. The line should be drawn, however (and this is only my opinion), at games of chance that have clear implications of gambling. My reason is twofold.

First, gambling appeals to the lower and less desirable traits of people. It is the age-old desire to get something for nothing. Nowhere in the Bible are we encouraged to exercise our faith by turning to games of chance to fund the ministries of the church.

Second, the churches that do choose to go this route have, in many cases, found themselves relying on bingo, Las Vegas nights, and other similar events to subsidize the ministries of the church. It may take time, but the temptation over the years is to allow these types of events to substitute for the offering plate. It has been my experience that

17. Hales, "The Role of Stewardship in the Local Church," in *Money for Ministries,* 101.

the churches that don't have a well-defined stewardship policy in this area or that are struggling financially (these may be mutually related) are the ones that rely on these types of events to fund their church operating expenses. I believe that state lotteries have proven this to be true. The states where lottery funds pay educational expenses have come to rely heavily on the proceeds from the lottery. Instead of local school districts or state governments budgeting carefully in order to make education a priority, they have depended on lottery proceeds while using general tax revenues for other purposes.

Improper fund-raising methodology can also create a sense that things aren't quite right. A crisis in confidence creeps in after several of these activities. First, people are asked to kick in money for a garage sale sponsored by the young married class. Then, the third graders put on a candy sale, followed by a college ministry car wash. Church members begin to grow weary of these appeals, not to mention that members may support these types of activities to the exclusion of their regular giving.

There is another problem associated with multiple fund-raising events—resentment. When a church conducts these events on a regular basis, people begin to support them grudgingly. Church members are confronted at Bible studies and youth groups, as well as in front of the church, by people selling tickets or other objects. Members will usually support these activities out of a sense of loyalty or duty; but often out of a sense of obligation they spend money on things they normally wouldn't buy. Then a feeling of resentment develops because people buy something they don't want just to support the church.

Many churches have a policy whereby they simply don't allow any fund-raisers. The leaders believe that, if the ministry is a worthy endeavor, the church as a whole should support it and back it with funds. The policy, therefore, is that church ministries will be funded through the church budget. If people don't want to support it through the budget, it is removed from the budget. Large fund-raisers designed to make up deficits or to support pet projects are eliminated.

The churches that feel that these activities are harmful may establish a policy to prohibit them. Arthur DeKruyter, pastor of Christ Church of Oak Brook, Illinois, says, "If a church has a tradition of fund raisers, it would be best to wean the congregation from them, slowly grafting those causes into the church budget. And if people won't put them into the church budget, well, a church may want to evaluate if those are significant ministries."[18]

Church leaders need to decide what methods of fund-raising will be used in their church and under what conditions. If there are to be any exceptions, what will they be? The basic policy is guided by the type, timing, and appropriateness of each of these events. Without these guidelines, each specific method of fund-raising that presents itself will become its own obstacle to an effective overall stewardship program.

18. Arthur DeKruyter, *Mastering Church Management* (Portland: Multnomah, 1990), 95.

Chapter 9

Is the Way We Give Hurting Our Church?

A note found in the offering plate read, "The enclosed check for $500 is to go toward the purchase of a new church organ." Also, Mr. Green, a regular tither, is now requesting that his weekly gift be sent to the hungry children in Ethiopia. In addition, Joe Youngblood, the youth pastor, received a gift of $100 from an anonymous donor: "In appreciation for your tireless efforts in working with our young people."

All those gifts are certainly appreciated, but what should church leaders do if they don't need a new organ or know of a way to get money to Ethiopian children? And maybe the youth pastor just got a raise. The church doesn't want to return the gifts, and yet the donors have placed certain conditions on the way church leaders should spend them.

Donations given to the church with specific instructions for their use, commonly known as "designated gifts," cannot quietly be added to the general fund and spent for current needs. Both the Internal Revenue Service and the donor have a legal and moral right to know exactly how a designated gift is spent. Gifts designated for mission projects, "love offerings" for speakers, donations to meet financial needs of church members, and funds given to finance concerts, musicals, films, radio programs, and scholarships for camps and schools all must be carefully accounted for.

Perhaps you like to earmark your giving so that you have control over where it is spent. But place yourself in the position of the church treasurer, who with each designated gift faces a bittersweet dilemma: How can he deal with the gift in a way that is agreeable to the donor, consistent with the purposes of the church, and in keeping with guidelines of the IRS and the principles of wise stewardship?

The wise treasurer asks two sets of questions:

1. Is the direction of this gift in line with the priorities of our church? If not, should we reevaluate our priorities in order to pursue the objective of the giver?
2. If we return the gift, what effect will our refusal have on the donor? How can we best handle our refusal?

If the gift is to an individual on the church staff, two additional concerns need to be addressed.

One has to do with fairness to other church employees. Staff members in positions of high visibility tend to receive more special gifts. But men and women working in support areas will have needs just as great—and possibly even greater, depending on their family situation. Is the church prepared to give them matching gifts?

The second concern is that the donor needs to know that a gift designated to an individual is not tax deductible. The law states, "If contributions . . . are earmarked by a donor for a particular individual, they are treated, in effect, as being gifts to the designated individual and are not deductible."[19] The treasurer may determine that a designated gift cannot be utilized in the way it was intended. As painful as it may be, he must openly and honestly talk to the person offering the gift, tactfully encouraging him to continue in his spirit of generosity by helping the church leaders meet the priorities and goals of the church.

Indeed, a deeper issue is at stake than the legal mechanics of handling designated gifts. The biblical concept of church leadership may be threatened by designated giving. Acts 4:35 sets forth a rather subtle yet profound practice. New Testament believers were truly committed to meeting the needs of others, but, instead of giving gifts directly to certain individuals or special projects, they would lay their gifts "at the apostles' feet, and they would be distributed to each as any had need."

The apostles were godly men with a proven track record of being good stewards. They were in a position to know the needs and requirements of the local body. As the God-ordained leaders of the body, they determined where and how resources were to be spent. It wasn't a case of a small group of powerful men trying to call all the shots. They were honest, trustworthy men, properly motivated, who knew where and how to get the job done. And the people confidently submitted to their leadership. The modern-day application of that first-century practice is threefold.

First, the responsibility of church finances should be placed in the hands of trusted, duly appointed leaders. Biblical church leadership is not by majority rule. Decisions—financial and otherwise—should be made according to the wisdom of godly church leaders who are charged with the responsibility of overseeing the entire congregation.

Second, establish an annual budget that provides funds for all the church ministries—a "unified budget." Here, different ministries are kept separate for internal bookkeep-

19. Internal Revenue Service, Ruling 62–113 (1962).

ing purposes. The fund for the new organ, the debt reduction funds, the camp scholarship fund, and the myriad of other special emphasis areas that tend to encourage designated giving can be allowed for on a limited basis in this way. If the church leaders recognize a specific area of need, they bring that need before the people of the church to request designated gifts.

Finally, establish a written policy limiting the solicitation and receiving of gifts for designated purposes. A suggested policy might read something like this:

> Contributions will not be received that are designated for organizations or individuals not recognized by the IRS as tax-exempt.
>
> Contributions can be designated for particular purposes, programs, or projects of the church itself, which have been duly authorized in advance as part of its religious activity by the Board of Elders (or your particular ruling body). Expenditures of such contributions for the purposes designated will be entirely within the discretion of the church or its appropriate internal body.
>
> If the church cannot find a way to utilize such contributions within its own purposes and the donor's designation, it will return the donation to the donor with an explanation of the problem.
>
> The church will determine the best means of carrying out its purposes with such contributions. If an outside agency is utilized, the church will continue to exercise expenditure accountability to make sure that its funds are applied to its purpose by any contractor, agent, or grantee.

In the final analysis, the practice of designated giving not only drains away from the church's financial base but also sets up a framework in which people can, in fact, "vote" with their checkbooks. In some situations, the church may be struggling just to pay the light bill or the minister's salary. A new stained-glass window simply may not be one of the pressing priorities. But the decision should be made by the church's spiritual leaders, not the people who have the most money.

Whether you agree or disagree with this approach, it certainly is something to think about!

Chapter 10

Hey, Brother, Can You Spare a Dime?

Former President Reagan once proposed, "If every church and synagogue in the U.S. would adopt ten poor families beneath the poverty level . . . we could eliminate all government welfare in this country."

Former New York City Mayor Edward Koch asked the 350 churches and synagogues of his city to shelter ten homeless men and women each night. His proposal was criticized by priests, rabbis, and ministers. He received only seven positive replies.

A *Wall Street Journal* article spotlighted the situation. It stated that churches throughout the country face increasing demands to help the impoverished. This dilemma is a growing concern among America's congregations.

The challenge to church leaders is clear: *We need to respond biblically.* We simply cannot sidestep the issue and hope it will go away. It's here—at our doorstep.

Needy people will call the church, arrive in broken-down cars, or walk in the front door. They all have the same request—food, a place to sleep, clothing, or gasoline. There is the young man who comes to the church asking for food and a place to spend the night. Another man in the congregation, who has been unemployed for two months, calls and says his family doesn't have enough food for the week.

Historically, this was once the church's responsibility—providing aid to the poor, aged, and disabled. But the church, for whatever reasons, allowed government to take over this burden. Now, because of cuts in various federally funded assistance programs, people are again turning to the church for help.

Although politicians expect churches to care for the needy, most congregations are not prepared to cope. They either have limited resources or simply do not feel obligated to help the poor.

The church has three options:

1. *Help everyone.* Provide food, shelter, and clothing to anyone who can demonstrate an apparent need and then allow God to deal with the question of their "honesty."
2. *Help no one.* The philosophy of "us four—no more—shut the door" is typical in today's churches. Parishioners believe that the problem is beyond the ministry and scope of the local church.
3. *Help the truly needy.* The ideal is to help these people become self-sufficient without creating a dependency on the church or just another welfare system.

In aiding the poor, we need to answer three questions to develop a clear-cut strategy.

Who Qualifies for Aid?

The Bible classifies two types of individuals. Hebrews 13:2 tells us, "Do not neglect to show hospitality to strangers, for by this some have entertained angels without knowing it."

Also, in 1 John 3:17 we read, "Whoever has the world's goods, and sees his brother in need and closes his heart against him, how does the love of God abide in him?"

We are responsible to help strangers and those in Christ's body. In setting priorities, Scripture tells us to "do good to all men, and especially to those who are of the household of the faith" (Galatians 6:10). Our first obligation is to God's redeemed family.

Who Do We Consider Needy?

Generally speaking, we need to respond to those without resources or an immediate ability to help themselves. First Timothy 5:5 describes needy widows as destitute, lacking a means for support. They're the ones devoid of basic necessities, "without clothing and in need of daily food" (James 2:15).

Resources include assistance from family, relatives, and friends (1 Timothy 5:4). Property, savings accounts, cars, television, or any other surplus items can be exchanged for basic provisions.

People worthy of aid, therefore, are those lacking necessities or the immediate ability to remedy their situation.

To What Extent Should We Meet Needs?

The answer, although simple to say, is difficult to implement. We have to meet immediate needs while helping individuals become self-supporting. Giving food without guidance encourages people to return whenever they get hungry. But there are many practical solutions.

Church members can donate nonperishable food items, clothing, and blankets for the needy. Gift certificates purchased from local supermarkets or fast-food restaurants also help.

One way to handle the situation is to allow a person to work for his money. The Bible says if a man won't work, he shouldn't eat (2 Thessalonians 3:10). Handing a man a paintbrush or shovel is a sure way to check out his motivation.

The local church can use public agencies, usually funded by private donors, to help those outside its congregation. The Salvation Army, rescue missions, halfway houses, the Travelers Aid Society, and other organizations are equipped to aid the distressed.

When money is given, it must be handled carefully. Cash might not be used for its intended purpose. Examine the genuineness of each person's request.

Since church members have worked hard to earn funds for purchasing provisions, church leaders must guarantee good stewardship. To ensure that you are not being "taken," prepare an interview questionnaire. The guide on the following page is designed to help church leaders determine a person's identity, employment status, possible church affiliation, and any additional resources he may have overlooked.

American churches cannot completely replace the nation's welfare system. Government should not throw its poor on the local church, saying, "Here, we can't afford these people anymore; you take care of them." We're committed to helping truly needy people so that they can eventually help themselves. That includes serving spiritual food as well as physical sustenance. Let's not neglect this aspect of our "aid program" by pouring all our time and resources into only meeting physical needs. Quoting Deuteronomy 8:3, Jesus said, "Man shall not live on bread alone, but on every word that proceeds out of the mouth of God" (Matthew 4:4).

Exhibit 10–1

Request for Assistance
Mountain Community Church

1. Are you a church member? If not, how were you referred to us?

2. What is your need? (Please be specific.)

3. Where do your closest relatives live?

4. Do they know about your need?

5. Are you receiving any aid (financial or otherwise) from a government agency (unemployment insurance, social security, worker's compensation)?

6. Have you been employed locally? Where?

7. When and where was the last time you sought employment?

8. Are you willing to work today if we know of an available job?

9. Do you attend church? If so, where?

10. What is your minister's name?

11. Have you sought assistance at any other churches in this area? If so, where?

12. If we are *unable* to help you, what other options do you have?

13. If we are *able* to help you, how many people are involved? (Please list family members or dependents.)

14. Do you have some form of identification?

(Please remember, our church is not a government-assisted agency. All available resources are a result of direct donations from our congregation.)

Chapter 11

How to Turn Around a Financially Troubled Church

Every day it seems the phone rings with people wanting their bills paid. Donations aren't keeping up with expenses. And to make matters worse, two of your key staff people quit to take better paying jobs elsewhere.

Even the pastor's appeal letters have lost their appeal! They sound like they were written in a bomb shelter during an air raid. Every other word is underlined in red. The tone is urgent, more serious: "Send money now; we've got a major crisis here!"

Sound familiar? You may be trying to manage a church experiencing similar problems. These can be hard and discouraging times.

To begin with, we need to *identify* a financially troubled organization. This is necessary to prevent problems from occurring and to highlight those areas that may lead to further difficulties. What are the signs that a serious problem exists? Generally speaking, if two or more of the six questions listed below require a yes answer, you need to take a close look at your ministry's financial health. They are "red flags" that tell us something is wrong.

1. Is income from donations less this year than last year?
2. Is it necessary to withhold payroll occasionally due to lack of funds?
3. Are you behind in payments to your vendors more than sixty days?
4. Are you borrowing against a line of credit in order to pay operational expenses?
5. Are you delaying purchases of essential goods and services?
6. Are you holding off on needed repairs and maintenance?

There is no simple, quick-fix formula that always works to reverse these situations. However, there are a few proven principles and methods that can turn around a financially troubled ministry. Consider these points and think about how they apply to your church. Some of these recommendations may seem drastic, but there are, no doubt, churches today that are in all stages of difficulty. Some may be skirting the edge of trouble, while others are fighting for their very survival. (If your church is in neither of these positions, you might want to file this information away for future reference.)

A fundamental question ought to be asked at the outset of any discussion like this: Should this ministry even continue to stay in existence? That is, is it still fulfilling its mission statement? Perhaps the unthinkable should be examined—instead of a turn-around, maybe a shutdown is more appropriate. There is always the option of merging with another church, and this should be taken seriously. As unusual as it may seem, this is one way to keep the purpose of the ministry functioning and to maintain member friendship networks. A complete redirection or emphasis is another option that should be explored.

In the final analysis, these questions should be posed: Is this ministry still financially viable? Is it going to make it?

There are those organizations, however, that are experiencing an opposite problem—rapid growth. This can be just as troublesome if not managed properly. You can end up building and staffing for explosive, temporary growth and then experience some painful cutbacks and layoffs down the road. Many major churches in the country have gone through some rather severe reductions as a result of a period of fast growth followed by declining revenues.

Before considering some of the specific measures required to hold off a further financial decline, review some of the primary characteristics of a nonprofit organization. This is important because it sets down some basic guidelines and philosophy.

The term *nonprofit*, when it is applied to an organization, conjures up different meanings to different people. For some people, *nonprofit* may mean "charitable, tax-exempt, publicly owned, or a prohibition against 'making money' from operations."[20]

Nonprofit organizations originally got their names because their operations were for the most part guided by motives other than monetary gain, or "profit." However, in general this title has tended to confer a significant misunderstanding concerning their operation among outsiders and, surprisingly, even among their own managers, especially those people who are appointed or elected to their governing bodies.

For example, many church boards would have a difficult time with their church ending a fiscal year with a surplus—they want the church to break even. They believe nonprofit means just that—no operating cash surplus. The fact of the matter is, generating cash surpluses may be the only way a certain church can survive and expand its base and ability to function effectively.

20. Richard F. Wacht, *Financial Management in Nonprofit Organizations* (Georgia State Univ. Business Publication, 1984), 20.

As Richard Wacht explains, "An organization must be financially solvent and maintain adequate liquidity in order to continue to operate; hence, it should, to whatever extent its governing board chooses, support itself out of operating cash surpluses."[21] It is at this point that many Christian organizations get into trouble. The practice of not having adequate cash reserves both to meet emergencies and to grow isn't given a high priority.

There is a second major reason churches have financial difficulties. It involves the leadership structure. Most churches philosophically operate with a *dual* "management structure." That is because their very nature and survival relies on simultaneously achieving two distinct objectives.

The first goal could be called a *professional* goal. For example, a mission organization generally exists to recruit, train, and send workers. A church is called to reach and make disciples of all people. You could call these public or professional goals.

A second type of goal for a church is to set forth *financial* objectives that are designed to meet the *professional* objectives. Without proper financial planning and control to ensure that cash is available to support the public goals, even the most high-sounding, worthy purposes will fail.

These two sets of goals must be met simultaneously—that is, one cannot take precedence over the other. And it is at this exact point that many organizations, especially churches, have difficulty. I call this a conflict between the "visionaries" and the "bottom-liners." If either mind-set prevails, the effectiveness of the organization will suffer.

One fundamental fact remains. It is a lot easier to raise funds when you can point to a record of professional success coupled with a good track record of fiscal responsibility.

When a church extends itself beyond its capability to meet its obligations, it may be viewed by the public as inefficient or tolerant of poor management. That impression then translates into a drop in donations, which results in cash-flow problems.

A professionally well-conceived program that fails to have good financial planning will produce the same result as a well-financed but poorly conceived professional program. The net effect is that the public will withhold its giving. Let's examine some of the specific steps that could be taken to eliminate some of the "red flags" mentioned earlier.

Maintain Credibility

The key word here is *integrity*. First, you want credibility with your donors, next with your suppliers, and then with your employees. Ask yourself and your key people three things:

21. Ibid.

"How do we represent ourselves to the public, to our suppliers, and to our employees?"

"Do people perceive us in a positive light?"

"What do people reasonably expect of our ministry?"

If you make promises to your donors, suppliers, or employees, you absolutely must deliver on them. Otherwise, your credibility will slip at an increasingly faster rate.

Control the Flow

You don't need to be a rocket scientist to figure out that cash flow is a major factor in the health of an organization. Herb Adler may have said it all: "Happiness is positive cash flow." For our purposes, it isn't simply happiness we want but *survival*. Survival is positive cash flow!

Time is not necessarily on your side in a cash-poor situation—therefore, certain steps need to be taken to accelerate a positive response. What I mean by this is that you need to move fast to close the payables-versus-receivables shortfall.

The treasurer or financial officer should have hands-on involvement with payables. He needs to allocate the limited financial resources available to him. We have a Christian moral responsibility to pay what we owe. The first priority is to make payroll, utilities, and rent. Perhaps you are forced to deal with new suppliers, which may mean you are on a COD basis. These need to be paid as well.

One person, the highest finance officer, should personally review the payables. Make partial payments to those vendors that fall within the following profile:

- Provider of vital goods or services
- "Wolf at the door"—a vendor who is threatening to "blow your house down" with threats of aggressive collection proceedings
- Vendors whose survival is being threatened by late payments and who can't make payroll because your church owes them so much

Another strategy is to examine those ministries or departments that are at best marginal. Some may no longer be functioning in the best interests of the church. You may have what's called a "cash cow"—a ministry or department that consumes a lot of cash but doesn't give very much "milk" in return. If so, it may be time to switch cows.

Freeze Hiring

No one is added to the staff or replaced at this point. This may mean that job descriptions get changed and that some people will have to hold dual positions. It may also be necessary to cut hours. The point of such drastic steps is that you absolutely must gain control over your cash resources and spending.

Get Usable Information

This is important. Examine the information being provided from various departments.

- Accounting information needs to be timely.
- Donor records should be accurate, with up-to-date postings.
- If leaders get a lot of reports that they really don't need or have time to read, stop having them prepared.
- Also, have some of the reports prepared in summary format rather than with a lot of supporting detail data.

Quite simply, the information must have a use and be accurate. Otherwise, it is not needed. Also, if the data isn't trustworthy, take whatever steps are necessary to improve it.

Communicate the Situation to Employees

"I've got good news and bad news," the pilot reported over the loudspeaker. "The bad news is, we've been lost for over an hour. But the good news is that, due to a strong tail wind, we're really making good time." Is that the situation your church faces? If so, deal with the bad news right away.

Call a meeting of the key leaders, department heads, and whoever else needs to attend. Explain to them the problems the church is having. Then ask them to tell you the best and worst aspects of the church. Let them vent their opinions—but *listen!* Listen for the general morale level. Listen to those people who are outspoken, both the positive and the negative people. Ask them what they would do if they were in your position right now. Ask them what it is this ministry does best. Then repeat back those positive points the people just voiced. Point out the positive—highlight it, emphasize it! Then never look back or bring up the negative again.

Next, call a meeting of the rest of the employees. Recite to them some of the bad reports you've heard and then move on to the positive characteristics of the church. Tell them some good news! This should be followed by a time to encourage the staff to submit their suggestions on how things can be turned around.

Adopt a Motto

Develop a slogan or motto—something upbeat and, again, positive.

A good example is the story of Doolittle's Tokyo raid during World War II. Jimmy Doolittle trained a hand-picked group of pilots to fly B-25 bombers off the deck of an aircraft carrier—something totally unheard of until then. These brave men flew the bombers to Japan and bombed Tokyo. The actual damage wasn't nearly as significant as the psychological effect on the Japanese people, not to mention the effect on the American soldiers' morale. Tokyo, the capital city and the home of the emperor, had been bombed by the enemy. Jimmy Doolittle got a lot of "bang for his buck"! The point of this illustration is that you need to find some type of psychological lift for your church.

Consider a Change in Image

Take a good look at your church's logo. When was the last time it was changed or modernized? Perhaps the stationery needs a face-lift. Also, have the receptionists answer the telephones with a different greeting.

Suggest that someone other than the pastor communicate financial needs to the congregation.

Why not ask the chairman of the board of the church to write and sign the next appeal letter?

Pick a specific, successful ministry or activity within your professional area and focus attention on it. Let your donors know what you are doing in a positive light—give them some good news.

We want to project a new, fresh image and not a picture of an organization with serious financial problems.

Develop an Action Plan

It's been said many times, but it's worth repeating: "Fail to plan—plan to fail." Most successful ministries have some form of strategic planning. At the minimum, this may consist of an annual operating plan consisting of projected income statements, balance sheets, cash-flow statements, capital budgets, and supporting schedules. Churches that have developed their planning process further include some sort of long-range plan.

Aside from the obvious fact that we want to get the church out of financial trouble, there are basically three major reasons for preparing an action plan:

1. Benefits are derived from the actual planning activity itself.
2. The plan provides a basis for measuring actual financial results against projections.
3. The plan acts as a vehicle for communicating to others what it is the ministry is trying to accomplish.

If the "red flags" mentioned earlier are present in your organization, a short-term plan needs to be developed. You can't just sit back in a reactive mode and allow the next crisis to hit. A game plan should be set forth to begin the turnaround process. What if giving drops another 5 percent? What if giving increases 10 percent? What is the first and second action you should take in response?

Furthermore, it is healthy to be forced to put down on paper where the ministry is in terms of what it has to offer, its donor base, and its relative "competitive" position in the donor market. Perhaps you may think that being competitive is unspiritual. But the facts are that your base of donor support has other ministries and appeals competing for its dollars. Local churches can suffer because of appeals from mission agencies, TV and radio ministries, and other Christian organizations. It isn't right, but it still happens. Church members should support these organizations out of "over and above" giving, but realistically it doesn't always happen that way.

Also, the ministry's financial requirements and the resources needed are important. It's possible to use what's called a "break-even chart." It's important to determine how much money it takes to keep an organization alive. You might want to do a little research into how one of these charts is prepared and what it could show you. A short-term action plan is a must for a church in need of a turnaround.

Generate New Cash

A. Sell Assets

This is the most bitter pill of all to swallow. Having to cut back can be viewed as God removing His blessing from your church. But who does the ministry belong to? Are you the owner of the organization or simply the manager? How you answer those questions will determine whether you are willing to let go of those things that are no longer necessary to the life of the ministry.

Depending on how serious the condition, you need to do whatever is necessary to save the ministry. There are many reasons why God may want the work to be smaller—the greatest of which may be because you or your board want it to be big. Think about it! Assets may include equipment, buildings, vehicles, computers—whatever isn't absolutely vital to the ministry may have to be sold.

B. Reduce Inventories

Next, you need to start to squeeze or cut inventories of supplies. This means reorder points should be reduced. I knew of one church that ordered large amounts of paper goods because they felt the suppliers would eventually cut them off for slow payment.

First of all, as a church, you really shouldn't buy something without a sure way of paying for it. That isn't the biblical model. Second, if the supplier is vital to your ministry, why destroy the relationship? Order in smaller quantities so you can pay the supplier more often. This will keep a better flow of materials and save a supplier from refusing to deal with you.

It also might be necessary to identify those items that are hardly used and eliminate them from the inventory.

C. Collect Your Receivables

Another obvious way to generate cash is to collect your receivables. For those of you involved in managing churches, the term *receivables* may sound like something only businesses have to contend with. However, a church might have two areas that could be considered receivables. If a pledge program is used, the people should be encouraged in a tasteful and sensitive way to be consistent with their financial commitments.

If the church has a day school, unpaid tuition is a receivable. Consider sending out a statement each month. Also, an interest charge on unpaid balances is appropriate here. Use some compassion, though, for there are single mothers and others who have genuine financial struggles of their own. If you adopt a late-penalty procedure, the parents should have thirty to forty-five days advance notice of this new policy. The monthly statements should then be aged in thirty-day increments.

A school also needs to have a written policy on how to handle delinquent accounts. Again, mail it to all parents with an appropriate amount of lead time.

If your ministry bills for goods and services, a standard accounts receivable collections procedure should be established. This would include delinquent notices that go out in a regular, periodic fashion.

Get Some Help

One final suggestion is to seek outside help. None of us has all the answers. Furthermore, lack of time often doesn't allow the luxury to reinvent the wheel. You don't want to repeat mistakes or go off on paths that could, in the long run, make matters worse.

There are fine Christian organizations and individuals throughout the country that could offer help. At a minimum, get a good accountant involved so you will get a clear perspective on the financial picture.

Experts are available in areas of fund-raising, organizational management, data processing, and so forth. Call them, tell them your situation, and don't be afraid to ask them how much it would cost for their services.

In conclusion, turning around a financially troubled ministry is no easy task. You will need complete cooperation from the senior pastor, the leadership of the church, and the employees of the ministry. Everyone should know that they may need to make some sacrifices. Also, many of the philosophies and methods of the past may need changing. Cooperation and flexibility are the key words. Without these, no turnaround will take place, and the church will be back where it was—only in deeper trouble.

Further, keep in mind that, once a ministry is restored to a healthy footing, it needs to stay there. Hopefully, whatever caused the problems in the first place has been identified and dealt with.

The next step, however, is to prevent it from recurring in the future. That is where the action plan referred to earlier comes into play. It's time to switch from a short-term mode to a more long-range outlook. That means more than just making plans for the future. It also involves putting in place internal controls and checkpoints that will identify those "red flags" before they make it to the top of the flagpole.

Churches having financial problems do little to advance the cause of Christ. The entire tone and direction of the ministry, as well as the testimony to the outside community, suffers. Churches owe it to their suppliers, employees, and donors—and, above all, they owe it to Christ—to keep their ministries headed in the right direction.

Section 3
Church Facilities

Chapter 12

Managing the Church Office

Is the church office basically for business or mainly for ministry? To say that the function of the church office is varied and multipurpose is an understatement. Nevertheless, the church office plays a unique part in the life of the local church. It is a necessity for carrying out certain business functions on a routine basis, but it is often a rallying point for church members, not unlike the country store in times past. In periods of great need and crisis, as well as during happier times, people gather in the church office to interact socially. It is a place where church workers, salaried or volunteer, stop by to socialize, to use office equipment, or to attend meetings.

The church office is often too small, ill-equipped, and improperly utilized.

> On an average Sunday morning approximately thirty million adults, age eighteen and over, will attend worship in a Protestant church in the United States. Nearly one-third of them will be present in congregations in which the average attendance is under 100, slightly over 30 percent will worship with congregations in which the attendance averages between 100 and 200, and approximately 38 percent will worship in churches that average more than 200 at worship.[22]

What this means when translating into floor space is that a high percentage of the churches in America are operating in fairly small facilities with perhaps less than adequate office space.

The business/ministry center of a church has four main needs: a purpose, a place, people, and procedures. The wise pastor will recognize these requirements and work to integrate them into a smooth-running organization.

The Purpose

The mission or purpose of a church office should reflect the behavior of the organiza-

22. Lyle E. Schaller, *The Middle-Sized Church: Problems and Prescriptions* (Nashville: Abingdon, 1985), 7.

tion—to care for the needs of people, both inside and outside the church family. At the same time, the office must perform necessary business functions. The people who work in the office thus have the dual roles of Christian ministry and sound business practice. Obviously, a minister has different duties than a secretary or bookkeeper, but the overall goal is the same.

With that in mind, church employees need to have a "customer orientation" about their work, a ministry-team concept. Telephone calls and walk-in interruptions are viewed as a part of the job and not as sources of irritation. The attitude should not be "I can't get my work done because I have all these people calling me." Rather, "all these people" *are* the work of the ministry.

The responsibility to keep the office running smoothly and on schedule often falls to the minister. The office may be staffed with no more than a part-time secretary giving a few hours a week, and the pastor himself may have to peck out the church bulletin each week and answer the phones for part of each day. Or the church may have a large, well-staffed administrative center equipped with state-of-the-art technology and highly trained personnel. However, whether the office houses a one-man operation or a staff of fifty, the mission remains the same—to serve the Lord and His people.

The Place

Church office space needs to be organized for the greatest efficiency and effectiveness. As a minimum, the minister should have a private office or a secluded work area. Such an arrangement provides a quiet study environment and a place for confidential meetings and counseling sessions. To allow for uninterrupted meeting or study time and for routine operations to continue, the church files should not be stored in the pastor's office.

The church secretary also needs to have a specific work area, located as close to the minister's office as possible. A wall or barrier—preferably a counter or chest-high wall—should separate the front entrance from the secretary's work area. This establishes a boundary for greater staff privacy and confidentiality.

The office environment should be planned around those functions that are basic to maintaining the communications of the church: bookkeeping, answering phones, corresponding, publishing materials, and so on. Once the required functions are identified, the physical aspects of the environment can be planned.

Acoustics

Noise created by office activities should not be allowed to disturb the staff's studying and counseling activities. Materials are available to make improvements in this aspect of the office environment. Acoustical conditions depend on ceiling, floor, wall, and window treatments. Where sound-producing equipment is located is also important. For example, avoid placing a computer printer next to a telephone.

Privacy

Acoustical privacy (a quiet place to work) is desirable, but so also is visual privacy. Screens or movable partitions can be used as visual barriers.

Lighting

Today's office needs to have adequate, effective, and energy-saving lighting. Glare can be a problem, especially on computer screens. The use of "work station" lighting is becoming more popular as a source of directed light, rather than depending exclusively on overhead lighting.

Carpeting

Carpeting can become a integral part of an office setting. It reduces both noise and maintenance costs. Carpeting also has aesthetic value. The criteria for selecting carpeting should define quality, color, wearability, pile height, and static-electricity avoidance.

Air-conditioning

Aside from the obvious comfort advantages, properly working air-conditioning can produce an acceptable level of humidity in an office. This actually helps office equipment operate better, particularly photocopiers, since the amount of moisture in the air affects the copier's handling of paper.

Equipment

In many cases, church office equipment may be obsolete, or the office may be under-equipped. An ideal situation would include the following:

- *Phone system.* A phone system with multiple extensions and features is within the price range of most churches. Some churches are even switching away from purchased equipment and returning to systems that are centrally located and maintained by the phone companies themselves. This eliminates many of the difficulties associated with servicing.
- *Facsimile (fax) machine.* This is a tool that, once used, causes one to wonder how he got along without it. An adequate fax machine is no longer a high-cost item.
- *Answering machine.* This type of equipment communicates our concern for keeping in touch with people. Many churches now record outgoing messages that give

church service times, special announcements, and a promise to call back if a message is left. Some communications companies also provide this type of service.

🗸 *Photocopier*. Buy a copier that fits your needs. The bells and whistles look good in the showroom, but how often will you actually need the additional features? For many churches, a collator is nice, but don't buy more machine than you need. One approach to need assessment is to count the number of copies your church makes in an average month, then add 25 percent to determine copy demand for your machine. Also, try to get at least three proposals from salespeople. Renting or leasing is also an option.

🗸 *Mail-room equipment*. A postage meter is convenient but can be expensive. It needs to be maintained and usually requires a maintenance contract. However, for those churches with a large mail volume, a meter can be a great time-saver.

Status

Although this may seem an inappropriate requirement for a church office, it still needs to be addressed. Aside from the needs for privacy as it relates to study, confidential meetings, and counseling, the rule of thumb for the assignment of space in offices with multiple staff should be confidentiality and protection of funds, not the establishment of rank. Staff who interact with the public a great deal should be accessible. Putting secretaries in private offices is usually not a good practice within church culture. However, putting a bookkeeper behind closed doors is certainly warranted.

Location

Few church facilities have the space needed to establish an efficient office environment. As a result, some churches are placing their offices off the church property. This leaves only the school (if one exists) and maintenance personnel on-site during the week, in addition to those involved in various (usually evening) ministries. This option has some noteworthy advantages: "Leased office space is more flexible and may be lower in cost than new construction and maintenance. In areas with low occupancy rates, significant rent reductions can be negotiated, especially for a church."[23]

The People

The largest category in any church's budget is usually the section relating to salaries and compensation. This is to be expected since a church is a people-oriented, hands-on type of organization. A pastor should be aware of this fact and not be concerned over what is considered the right percentage of staff compensation to the budget as a whole. There is no rule of thumb as long as the ministry needs are being met and the staff

23. Nick Nicholaou, "The Optimal Office," *Your Church* (July/August 1993), 18–19.

members are working hard and effectively. Though cash flow often dictates how many staff a church should have, other factors are more important considerations: expectations of the congregation, the availability of volunteers, and new ministry needs.

Staffing depends on the basic needs of the church. When a church grows and new ministries come on-line, more staff should be added. Though some churches add staff for growth, as opposed to increasing staff in response to growth, the cautious approach is to add positions as the needs arise. Overstaffing or adding positions in anticipation of growth, while it could be termed "stepping out in faith," isn't always for the best. Staff reductions due to insufficient funds are painful. Each new position needs to be evaluated carefully and responsibly before adding additional burdens to the church's financial commitments.

Before a new staff member is hired, his or her specific position should be identified. It can encompass multiple duties and even titles, but it must be made explicit. There should, therefore, be a written job description. It should be simple, clear, and not too narrow. The main features of a well-written job description are:

✔ Job title
✔ Responsibilities
✔ Brief description of duties
✔ Who the person answers to
✔ Who, if anyone, this person supervises (including volunteers)
✔ Basic requirements of the position
✔ Full- or part-time status and number of hours expected per week
✔ Working conditions, where appropriate

No matter what size the church staff, a personnel policy handbook is absolutely essential (see chapter 15). The need to set policy guidelines and rules and to be in compliance with federal and state laws makes a written policy a necessity. Employees also tend to work better in organizations that have set rules and standards. Many excellent resources are available to churches in this field. (See the resource section at the end of this chapter.)

As a church staff increases in size, it is desirable to establish an "office procedures handbook." Such a handbook contains standards for routine procedures, the use of specific stationery and format, where important papers, keys, and supplies are located, and, of course, who is responsible for which specific tasks in the office.

The Procedures

Some church members feel that the office, church employees, and the equipment are there for their personal use. Although, to a limited degree, the office resources should be made available for general church business, basic guidelines need to be clarified.

Three Important Rules

1. The minister's work has precedent over any other work given to the secretary. However, the minister can decide which projects have priority over others and may in some cases allow the secretary to work on an activity other than his.

2. If the church office has more than one secretary, an office manager should be appointed. All work should be channeled and prioritized through the manager. The receiving and managing of work flow and assignments through one person will help eliminate the problem of who does what for whom. If a board member or Sunday school teacher asks a secretary to do a certain job, the manager can serve as "traffic cop" regarding work-flow decisions.

3. Specific assignments should be given to specific people. For example, a church master calendar should be handled by one person, ordering supplies should be designated to another person, and so forth. It works best to divide up the regular duties and make assignments.

The Pastor-Secretary Interface

With the introduction of computers, many ministers are performing some tasks themselves. Word processing programs enable pastors to write their sermons faster. In addition, they can make use of electronic Bible dictionaries, concordances, and other resources. Whenever possible, however, the minister should allow the secretary to handle the office/clerical functions. In most cases, church members would prefer to have their pastor pastoring rather than typing!

Suggestions for Pastoral Efficiency

There are many ways to make an office more efficient and to make better use of the pastor's time. Time is a precious commodity, and the pastor needs to know how to use it effectively.

Keep a time log. Time study experts recommend using a log of daily activities in half-hour increments. Daily or weekly calendars are available through most stationery stores.

Consolidate activities. Rather than making many trips to the photocopier for single copies that are not urgent, wait until several items need copying and make the trip once. When the minister steps out of his study into the general office area, he often has many questions and requests for the secretary, and they tend to come all at once. It would be helpful if there were an "out basket" available for the secretary to check once an hour. That would cut down on the number of disruptions for both.

Handle routine tasks efficiently. Here again, pastors and secretaries can fall into routines that waste time. For example, handling mail is one great time-waster that needs to be controlled. It isn't necessary to read every letter thoroughly. Merely scan the letter and route it to the appropriate person. Some offices have cumbersome and outdated filing systems. There are excellent resources available to help in this area. *Merriam-Webster's Secretarial Handbook* is a good one. Another common problem involves the length of time various documents are filed or stored. How long do you need to hold on to an annual financial report? What about payroll journals or giving records? There are set rules for record retention. A useful booklet that answers these and other questions is listed in the resource section at the end of this chapter.

Make to-do lists. Like a calendar, a daily list of tasks and their priorities is important to keep you on track. It is best to prepare this list each night before you go home. Some experts suggest that you start the day with the routine tasks you least like. Getting them done and out of the way can be a morale booster, and you can look forward to the more pleasant tasks.

Know your limits. Don't try to be a super manager by saying yes to everyone. Get assistance or delegate whenever possible. Learn to say no, when appropriate, in a pleasant manner and without feeling guilty.

Avoid interruptions. Often, just the repositioning of a desk can cut down on the number of distractions. Does the desk in your office look directly out into the office area? Can people who enter the front door see you? Making eye contact is how an interruption often gets started. Also, a simple phone system with more than one station and a hold button works wonders in cutting down the number of direct phone calls to the minister. These calls can be intercepted and screened when necessary.

Let the computer help. The computer can provide many shortcuts in dealing with routine functions. The mail-merge feature in most software programs can save on the time it takes to personalize form letters. Many other time-saving features are built into these programs as well. Periodically read the software manual to pick up new labor-saving tips. A mailing-list program is a quick and easy way to remind people of meetings on a routine basis. Keep a separate file for each group, and simply run labels for those groups as needed. Many of the larger church software programs have special codes that indicate participation in various groups. A mailing can be produced in just minutes by having the computer select only those people who belong within specified groups.

Conclusion

It is certainly possible to create and manage an office that fills the need for a limited social setting as well as for the performing of church business. This can be accomplished only when each of the factors outlined in this chapter has been understood and set in place. The mission to serve God and His people is a worthy goal and one that deserves the time required to plan the ministry environment and the effort necessary to manage it on a daily basis.

Resource Guide

The Record Retention Guide (1984), available from the Christian Management Association, Diamond Bar, California.

The Personnel Policy Manual and Employee Handbook (1992), available from Alston-Kline, Inc., Edmonds, Washington.

For a custom-written personnel policy handbook, contact Ministry Business Services, Inc., in Huntington Beach, California: 1–717–847–4545.

Chapter 13

Managing the Facilities

An empty stable stays clean—but there is no income from an empty stable" (Proverbs 14:4 TLB*). If you apply that verse to church facilities, you would say, "If we could just lock all the Sunday school classrooms, the kids wouldn't mess them up!"

Obviously, that isn't a practical solution to managing facilities in a local church. Caring for facilities in today's church requires skill, creativity, hard work, and in some cases a great deal of diplomacy. Properly managing a church's buildings and grounds is an area that presents unique situations to each church.

Scheduling

The issue of scheduling is a logical place to start. As mentioned before, we could simply shut the buildings down and lock the doors to save money, along with wear and tear. If you pursue that notion to its logical end, then why have buildings at all?

In dealing with the issue of scheduling, it is best to have one central church calendar. There should also be one person who is designated "keeper of the calendar." This individual should be a "people person" and be firm but fair (objective, not playing favorites). Many churches reproduce their calendars and have them distributed on a periodic basis—weekly, biweekly, or monthly. It is not uncommon even to publish a three-month calendar.

An easy way to help people get room reservations on the calendar is to provide a simple sign-up form. The form should be uncomplicated yet inclusive. Above all, it should be in at least two parts—a copy for the church and one for the member. A sample form is provided at the end of this section. (See Exhibit 13–1.)

The Living Bible.

The calendar contact person should communicate frequently with the head custodian. A room may be in need of repair, and you certainly don't want activities planned in a room that is being painted.

Usage

Every church should have a basic set of guiding principles relating to the use of its facilities. Time, setting, and proximity are to be considered in the overall policy and scheduling process.

Time

The time of day is important because it may affect other activities. What other similar or conflicting event is taking place at the same time? Scheduling the high school music group and a high school party at the same time hurts both activities.

Setting

The activity needs to be appropriate to the room or setting. You don't want an exuberant junior high party in the sanctuary or a pie-eating contest on a carpeted area (if possible). Appropriateness has to do with both taste and the potential mess likely to result from the activity.

Proximity

Having a band performing in a room next to the monthly Board of Elders meeting is not good scheduling. Although this is an extreme example, it is an illustration of the importance of proximity. The basic principle, therefore, is simply to make sure the time of day, the appropriateness of the setting, and the proximity to other groups is considered.

Maintenance

Once again, many maintenance issues relate specifically to each church and its buildings. But, as in the case of scheduling and usage, there are some standard guidelines.

It is possible to be creative in this area as well. For instance, does your church use its own people for maintenance and custodial work, or is it possible to contract it out? Another overall question would be, Do we want to hire people who are generalists, the "handyman" type of person, or do we focus on bringing in specialists to care for our buildings? Most churches cannot afford a staff of specialists, so they stay with a man with overall skills and call in a specialist when it is necessary. Electrical, heating, air-conditioning, plumbing, and some construction work often are done by outside contractors.

The same is true for custodial services. Many churches contract this out in order to avoid the cost of maintaining their own staff. The exception, however, is those churches that require multiple room setups and teardowns. Most custodial services will not set up chairs, platforms, podiums, microphones, and so on. It is usually best to hire your own people on a limited basis to perform these tasks and definitely to be available on Sundays.

Finally, the maintenance and care of buildings over the long haul is performed better if there is a scheduled routine. Churches with large facilities should rotate the carpet care and other ongoing routine maintenance on a periodic basis. There is always maintenance and upkeep work to be done on church facilities. A request for maintenance work should be submitted in writing and properly scheduled. (See Exhibits 13–2 and 13–3.)

Building Security

This has become a matter of great importance to most churches today. Unfortunately, churches have been notoriously poor at dealing with this issue. Some are learning the hard way that a church is an easy target for crime and vandalism. Generally thieves go after money, computers, office machines, sound equipment, anything that is portable and can be sold quickly. There is even an increase in malicious vandalism directed at churches in many areas of the country.

Because a church is a somewhat public building, it is difficult to have high security measures. ID badges and coded access doors with closed circuit cameras aren't always appropriate. So a good philosophy is "If it isn't nailed down, you'd better lock it up!"

Many churches today are scheduling much of their custodial work at night. For example, two shifts can be scheduled: 3:00–11:00 and 11:00–7:00. This allows the work to be accomplished when the buildings are empty. Further, the activity, with lights going on and off in different buildings during the night, provides a sense of security. Many churches are also using drive-by security services to check buildings and locks and even to ask the identification of people wandering around the buildings after hours. The goal is to have the church either look busy or be under surveillance as much as possible.

If that is not practical, install electronic measures to secure your buildings with window tapes, magnetic threshold contacts, motion detection, and heat-sensing devices. There are even churches that hire their own guards to walk "a beat" and keep an eye on buildings and grounds at night.

A further protective measure has to do with the issuing of keys. In many churches that can be a political "hot potato." However, everyone doesn't need to have access to buildings. Perhaps the best policy is to have your church's ruling board decide which people should get keys. Letting the board make this decision removes that burden from the senior pastor, church employees, or individual members.

Property Liability

In today's society, this is one area where your church could be financially wiped out in a very brief time. It isn't wise to cut corners when it comes to purchasing liability insurance. Needless to say, you would want to insure the buildings and contents for their replacement value as well as to identify the more significant areas of risk to your church property. There are many instances in which churches have discovered that their property was underinsured after a loss, resulting in a great deal of out-of-pocket expense. Once again, your chances of a loss from theft are significant, the reason being that a church is a somewhat public building with easy access and many visitors.

Another high-risk area involves injuries occurring on your property. Although this may seem like a legal matter and not a facilities issue, any hazard within reason that could cause an injury should be removed (see chapter 14). Special attention should be given to athletic events because the potential for injury increases, especially when equipment is poorly maintained or there are hazards present. Experience has shown that in today's environment some people will not hesitate to sue a church if they are injured.

Built for a Purpose

Finally, remember that church buildings belong to God and His people. They should be utilized to their fullest, keeping in mind the appropriateness and the need for balanced schedules. Just as an airplane was designed and built to fly, our church facilities must also fully meet their intended use and purpose—to help advance Christ's kingdom.

Exhibit 13–1
Activity & Calendar Request Forms

Room Number	**ACTIVITY & CALENDAR REQUEST FACILITY RESERVATION**

Name of activity _____

Date of function _____ From (am/pm) _____ To (am/pm) _____

Name of group_____ Contact Person_____

Phone (home) _____ (work)_____

Address _____ City_____ Zip _____

Number of people expected _____ Dept. head approval _____

Nursery care needed: yes/no   Bulletin announcement needed: yes/no

Reservations (tickets) needed: yes/no

Where _____ Cost $ _____ Deadline _____

Audio-Visual equipment needed _____

Other equipment needed _____

Food or refreshments served _____

VEHICLE REQUEST

Name of Group _____ Function _____

Destination _____

Van # _____ Date needed _____

Time (leaving) _____ (returning) _____

Program leaders are responsible for getting drivers, vehicle inspection forms, medical/liability consent forms, and van keys.

Use below for Room Set Up Diagram

MASTER CALENDAR

Today's Date _____

Time_____

Initials_____

White and yellow copies to Facilities Director; pink copy to Receptionist.

175

Exhibit 13–2
Work Order Request Form

FIRST CHRISTIAN CHURCH
<u>WORK ORDER REQUEST</u>

(Complete and submit to church office)

Requested by:_____ **Dept.:**_____ **Date:** _____

Room/Area where work is to be performed: _____

Description of services requested:* _____

_____

_____

***Use the back for further description or illustration.**

Work performed _____

_____

Signature:_____

For Office Use Only	
Material charge: _____ G/L #: _____	
Manhours to complete: _____ Date completed: _____	

Exhibit 13–3
Custodial Maintenance Daily Worksheet

	Time	Job #	Description of services requested:	✔
Custodial Maintenance Daily Worksheet	by: _____ Date: _____			
1.				
2.				
3.				
4.				
5.				
6.				
7.				
8.				
9.				
10.				
11.				
12.				
13.				
14.				
15.				
16.				
17.				
18.				
19.				
20.				

NOTES

Chapter 14

Managing the Risks

Many church members don't give much thought to the potential liability risks in their own church. After all, who would sue a church? On the other hand, since the American Bar Association in 1990 conducted workshops on how to sue churches and clergy members, local church congregations need to sit up and take notice. Religious organizations are no longer off-limits when it comes to lawsuits and liability injuries.[24]

Is your church financially protected if any of the following events should occur?

- Your building is damaged by fire
- An attender is hurt on your property
- An employee steals office equipment
- A car drives through your front doors
- The church treasurer embezzles a large sum of money
- A church employee is hurt on the job
- The church is burglarized
- The senior pastor dies

What would you do? The usual answer is, "Call our insurance agent." That is, of course, assuming you have insurance covering any or all of these claims. Relying on insurance is only one of many remedies.

Risk Management

There are four ways a church can cope with the possibility of claims arising from injury or other forms of liability.

---

24. Steve Levicoff (*Christian Counseling and the Law* [Chicago: Moody, 1991]) has written a good resource book for churches concerning contemporary legal realities.

Eliminate the Risk

It is possible to totally eliminate certain, specific risks. These could be related to employees using inferior materials or unsafe equipment. Moreover, perhaps your buildings are designed with hazardous walkways, low clearances, slippery surfaces, or other dangers. Then there are always the well-known hazards of faulty wiring, exposed steam pipes, broken stairs, and other areas demonstrating clear negligence. A church, like any other organization, risks the possibility of injuries and liability by not identifying and eliminating these problems. If church leaders don't take these potential hazards seriously, they could be exposed to lawsuits and, in some instances, could be criminally liable. Furthermore, gross negligence or flagrant violations of health and safety standards is sufficient cause for an insurance carrier to void and cancel your policy.

Lower the Risks

From a practical standpoint, it would be impossible to eliminate every risk, even if you knew where they were. So, short of total removal, the next best thing is to reduce the risks. Take a close, critical look at your church buildings and grounds to determine what, if anything, can be done to lessen possible hazards. What precautionary steps can be taken to reduce your exposure in these areas?

For instance, the danger of falling off a ladder cannot be eliminated; but the use of safety ladders with guardrails on either side can reduce the risk. Hallways need to be free of obstacles; walkways should be clear of electrical cords (overhead projector operators take note!). Having a good policy regarding the issuing of keys to buildings and protecting computers and office equipment from being carried away are examples of ways to reduce risks.

Accept the Risks

Self-insurance has been suggested in the past as one method whereby a church can create a contingency fund to pay for claims, instead of paying liability insurance premiums. Although that may have been an option in the past, it is no longer practical. The cost of legal fees, plus the size of a possible judgment, makes the practice of "going bare" totally impractical. Given high replacement costs for buildings, furniture, and fixtures, as well as the staggering amounts of some judgment claims, a church could be totally wiped out with one incident.

Accepting the risk can be appropriate when the risk cannot be totally eliminated or the cost of insurance is prohibitive. As any insurance agent will tell you, it is possible to buy insurance for almost every conceivable risk. But that simply isn't practical for most churches.

Furthermore, there are situations where, even though the church carries coverage for a specific risk, it may be advisable to go ahead and pay the damages. This applies when there is a likelihood that your premiums will increase significantly as a result of the incident or when the costs of the claim are within the policy's deductible portion.

Shift the Risk

Purchasing insurance coverage enables the church to transfer its risks. In effect, when you buy insurance, you agree to absorb some of the smaller, periodic losses in the form of premiums and deductibles in exchange for avoiding the larger, uncertain claims.

Types of Insurance

Fire Insurance

Most standard fire insurance policies cover the buildings, the property contained within them, and property temporarily removed from them because of fire or lightning. Normally, this coverage does not extend to accounting records, bills, deeds, money, securities, windstorms, hail, smoke, explosions, vandalism, automatic sprinkler leakage, or malicious mischief. A church needs additional coverage to guard against these losses. Fires resulting from a war or actions taken under the orders of a civil authority are not covered by insurance.

In order to keep your fire insurance policy valid, it is the church's responsibility to take every reasonable precaution to protect its property both before and after a fire. Aside from inspecting facilities for fire hazards, church leaders need to be aware of the type of activities going on in their buildings. Having an indoor barbecue, using unprotected candles, and cooking on a hot plate or a faulty pilot light are examples of preventable risks. Negligent acts such as renting your facility out to people who are neglectful or engage in reckless activities could void your coverage.

Liability Insurance

Church leaders are responsible for the safety of church employees as well as those who attend. Most liability policies cover losses stemming from bodily injury or property damage claims, expenses for medical services required at the time of the accident, investigation, and court costs.

These types of policies will pay claims depending on both the limit per accident and the limit per person provided for in the policy. For example, if your policy has a per-accident limit of $400,000 and a per-person limit of $100,000, and if one person receives a $300,000 judgment against the church, the insurance company will pay only $100,000. That means the church will be responsible for paying the balance of

$200,000, even though it is within the per-accident limit. Needless to say, the operative word here is "caution." In other words, read the fine print as well as the bold print and be sure you agree with any of the limitations in your coverage.

Automobile Insurance

If your church owns one or more vehicles, automobile insurance is essential. Coverage in this area should include the following:

- ✔ Bodily injury claims
- ✔ Property damage claims
- ✔ Medical payments
- ✔ Uninsured motorist damages
- ✔ Damage to your vehicles
- ✔ Towing costs

The cost of coverage normally depends on the value and number of vehicles and the kinds of driving involved (making deliveries, carrying passengers), as well as the location of the church. And of course, the higher the deductible, the lower the premium.

Worker's Compensation Insurance

The laws in every state require employers to (1) provide employees with a safe place to work, (2) hire qualified co-workers, (3) provide a safe work environment and tools, and (4) warn employees of dangerous working conditions. Failure to do this could result in liability damages. It is also quite possible that a worker could be paid for an on-the-job injury the rest of his life.

All churches are subject to worker's compensation laws, and this is not a case of government interference in religious affairs. In fact, it could be viewed as government protecting or absorbing some of the liability risks relating to employee injuries or disabilities. A church especially should want to provide a safe and secure workplace for its employees.

Under worker's compensation insurance, the carrier pays all claims the employer is legally required to pay a claimant. Basic insurance rates are set by law in most states, but a church can still control its premiums to a certain extent. Since rates vary according to the occupational category, make sure all church employees are classified correctly. You do not want an office worker classified along with the higher classified maintenance or custodial person. Another way to lower premiums is to ensure that safety measures are in place to reduce the risk of an accident and possible claim.

Management vs. Stewardship

There are other types of insurance a church may choose to purchase, although these are less significant. They include business interruption insurance, glass insurance, fidelity bonds, crime insurance, and key personnel insurance. A checklist of possible coverage is provided for your church to determine if you are adequately insured. (See Exhibit 14–1.)

Some believe that God will protect His church and that, therefore, it isn't necessary to purchase a lot of insurance. The Bible is clear that God does protect His people from a spiritual standpoint. In those instances, however, where God has given a local body of believers facilities and vehicles, He expects the leaders to be good stewards. Throughout the Old Testament, in those instances where God physically protected His people Israel, He still expected their cities to have walls, gates, and armed soldiers. That was the kind of world they lived in and the way they managed risks.

Today, in most locations, our church buildings don't require armed guards posted twenty-four hours a day. However, we make sure that the doors are locked, alarms set, strategic locations well lit, and liability insurance premiums paid in full. The world we live in sometimes requires added protection—even for churches. Good risk management is also good stewardship.

Exhibit 14–1
Insurance Checklist

Insurance Checklist

Type of insurance	Purchase	Do Not Purchase
Property insurance		
Fire	_____	_____
Windstorm	_____	_____
Hail	_____	_____
Smoke	_____	_____
Explosion	_____	_____
Vandalism	_____	_____
Water damage	_____	_____
Glass	_____	_____
Liability insurance	_____	_____
Workers' compensation	_____	_____
Business interruption	_____	_____
Dishonesty		
Fidelity	_____	_____
Robbery	_____	_____
Burglary	_____	_____
Comprehensive	_____	_____
Personal		
Health	_____	_____
Life	_____	_____
Key personnel	_____	_____

Section 4

Church Personnel

Chapter 15

Workers Worthy of Hire

It is not uncommon for a church today to spend at least 50 percent of its total annual budget on staff salaries. Furthermore, the total cost of employee compensation includes more than just the dollars spent on salaries. Other expenditures such as health and life insurance, workers' compensation, Social Security taxes, disability insurance, and retirement programs should be figured into the equation. When the total employee costs are calculated, it represents a major share of the church budget.

Yet, this is an area where many churches have difficulty. With that much money at stake, one would think that policies and reasonable practices would be set in place. But that is not always the case. It often isn't so much a problem of intent or neglect; it is simply not knowing what to do. Though Scripture says that "the laborer is worthy of his wages" (1 Timothy 5:18), it gets a little more complicated than that in today's society. Which laborers, under what conditions, full-time or part-time, exempt or nonexempt?

The whole field of personnel management has undergone so many changes in recent years that the business world has even given it a new name—Human Resources Development. Although the principle of a laborer being worthy of his wages is true (see Matthew 10:10), we need more specifics in dealing with church employees today.

Stewardship of financial resources extends from its beginning in the church member's pocket (actually it starts in the hand of God) to the manner in which the church staff is compensated. This flow of funds, however, requires some accountability, organization, and structure.

The initial step in this process should be the forming of a small group that, for lack of a better title, could be called the personnel committee. The function of this group is to set personnel policies, establish and administer an equitable compensation program, and act as a sounding board and a last resort in dealing with employee-related problems. The pastor could serve on this committee, but the rest of the group should be laypeople. This will ensure objectivity and openness.

The members of the personnel committee, under the authority of the church's ruling board, would be responsible for finding, interviewing, and recommending what, in their opinion, would be acceptable individuals for all paid staff positions. The exception would be the locating and recommendation of a senior pastor. Their duties would include the following:

1. Study the needs for future personnel
2. Develop and accurately adjust on an ongoing basis all position descriptions
3. Develop and maintain an organization chart and personnel policy
4. Locate, interview, and recommend to the church all employed staff personnel
5. Recommend to the board the salary and benefit program[25]

The personnel committee serves a vital role in the church. It has a significant part in determining how a large proportion of the church budget will be spent each year. These people need to be mature and sensitive, firm but fair in their deliberations.

Personnel Policy

Even if a church has only one employee—the senior pastor—it needs to have a policy relating to employment. Usually, as a church grows in size, the size of the staff grows with it. Personnel policies out of necessity also tend to grow in a corresponding fashion. The larger church will have a need to maintain organizational structure and avoid legal problems associated with employees. A small church simply needs to have in writing the basics of an employment policy.

Generally speaking, most personnel policies follow a standard format. Although the sample policy provided here may seem too complicated or appear to be directed toward a larger church and therefore inapplicable for small churches, simply use those portions that relate to your own church situation while discarding those that don't apply. You may also request a custom-written personnel policy handbook from Ministry Business Services, Inc., in Huntington Beach, California: 1–717–847–4545.

25. Mark Short, *Church Administration Handbook*, ed. Bruce Powers (Nashville: Broadman, 1985), 82.

Personnel Policy Manual

FIRST CHRISTIAN CHURCH OF LAKE CITY

Introductory Statement

Welcome to First Christian Church. We trust you will enjoy your work here and that we will be proud of you as a member of our staff.

In this booklet, we explain what the Church expects from you and what you can expect from the Church. We have tried to use simple, clear language to avoid misunderstandings. If any statement in this booklet is not clear to you, please feel free to ask questions.

We try to be careful to hire only those persons we feel reasonably sure are qualified to do the work of the Lord and who will be congenial with others working here. If we hire someone who will not or cannot do the work satisfactorily, it will be necessary to discharge him or her to permit the Church to fulfill its mission to serve Christ and our people.

We hope that you will find satisfaction in your work. May we both enjoy pleasant relations for many years.

This handbook puts into writing, in the same manner as a contract, what you can expect from First Christian Church and what is expected from you. We want you to call to our attention anything you feel is not right.

Classification of Employees

Pastoral Staff

Individuals who are responsible for major ministry responsibilities.

General Employees

Full-time personnel employed in support functions or as ministry directors. *Full-time* is defined as a permanent employee working a minimum of thirty-two hours per week.

First Christian Church uses the following terms as a basis for its payroll system and personnel administration:

Salaried Employees (Exempt)

Personnel paid on the basis of an annual salary and not subject to premium pay for overtime.

Hourly Employees (Nonexempt)

Personnel paid on the basis of an hourly rate and subject to premium pay for overtime. Hourly employees are full-time or part-time personnel.

Temporary Hourly Employee

An individual whose service is for a brief period of time. He or she may work part time, a regular forty-hour week, or be on call.

Evaluation Period

During the first ninety days of employment, each new staff member will meet several times with his or her direct supervisor for the purpose of monitoring job performance. At the end of this period, a formal performance appraisal will be discussed. Subsequently, you will receive a formal performance evaluation annually on your hire date anniversary.

Attendance

Every employee is expected to work all his or her scheduled hours, to report for work on time, and to work to the end of the work period.

If, for any reason, you cannot report for work on time, telephone the Church as far in advance of your starting time as possible. State why you will be absent and how long you expect to remain absent or late.

Absence for three consecutive work days without notification is considered job abandonment. Absence without approval is considered unexcused and will be subject to discipline.

An employee may be tardy three times per month before the Church will consider discharge or discipline due to habitual tardiness.

Change of Employee Status

Notify the church at once whenever there is a change in your

- Address
- Telephone number
- Person to notify in case of emergency, accident, or illness
- Name or marital status
- Number of dependents
- Insurance beneficiary

Group Insurance Program

Group insurance is offered as a part of the Church's benefit program for full-time employees. For the purposes of definition and unless otherwise approved, all provisions of the employee benefit program apply to full-time employees only. *Full-time*, for insurance purposes, is interpreted to mean thirty-two hours or more per week.

A brochure is available that outlines all the health and life insurance benefits available to full-time employees.

The cost of the insurance for you as an employee will be paid for by the Church.

Vacation Benefit

Vacations will be granted, with pay, to all full-time employees after one (1) year of continuous employment in the Church. The following conditions prevail:

1. Vacations may be accumulated up to a maximum of twenty (20) working days. Accrued vacation days may be carried from one twelve-month period to the next, up to a maximum of twenty (20) working days.

2. The amount of vacation granted will be on the basis of unbroken service with the Church.

3. Pay will not be given in lieu of unused vacation.

4. Employees who have worked less than one year but more than six (6) months can be entitled to prorated vacation time at the discretion of the appropriate supervisor.

5. Employees who resign from First Christian Church with proper advance notification (notice in writing two weeks prior to termination) and have completed one or more years of service will be entitled to earned vacation pay at the time of termination.

6. Employees who resign without giving proper notice, or who are discharged for cause, shall not be entitled to earned vacation pay.

Employees—Exempt and Nonexempt

All full-time employees shall be granted vacations based on tenure of employed service in the Church in accordance with the following services:

One (1) year and less than six (6) years	2 weeks
Six (6) years and less than eleven (11) years	3 weeks
Eleven plus (11 +) years	4 weeks

Pastoral Staff

Additional absences may be supported for local work at camps, tours, seminars, crusades, or conferences according to full-time maximums. All pay received in excess of expenses will be given to the church payroll officer.

Staff

First year	2 weeks
1–5 years of service	3 weeks
6–10 years of service	4 weeks
11–15 years of service	5 weeks

Pastor Advisory Level

0–5 years	4 weeks
6 years plus	5 weeks

Senior Pastor

0–5 years	4 weeks
(plus 2 weeks for outside meetings)	
6 years plus	5 weeks

Employees—Temporary

No paid vacation

Holidays

All full-time employees shall be granted the following ten (10) paid holidays per year.

> New Year's Eve (½ day)
> New Year's Day
> Good Friday (½ day)
> Memorial Day
> Independence Day
> Labor Day
> Thanksgiving Day and the Friday following
> Christmas Eve
> Christmas Day
> Floating holiday (to be designated by the employee)

Those full-time employees who are required to work on one of the designated holidays shall be granted compensatory time off.

If a holiday falls on a Saturday, it will be observed on the preceding Friday, and, if it falls on a Sunday, it will be observed the following Monday.

Sick Leave

Temporary employees and those working less than thirty-two (32) hours per week are not eligible for sick leave. Paid sick leave is granted to the following employees after six (6) months' service:

Sick leave shall accrue from the date of hire at the rate of seven (7) hours per month to a maximum of 120 hours. Employees starting from the first through the fifteenth of the month will accrue seven (7) hours for that month; employees starting the sixteenth through the end of the month will accrue three and a half (3½) hours for that month and seven (7) hours per month thereafter until the maximum is reached.

Accrued sick days may be carried over from one twelve-month period to the next up to a maximum of 120 hours in any twelve-month period.

Paid sick leave is to be used exclusively for the employee's personal illness, immediate family illness, or medical appointment.

Pay Periods

Paychecks are issued on the 15th and last day of each month. When payday falls on a Saturday or Sunday or a public holiday, paychecks will usually be issued on the preceding workday.

Hours and Attendance

The normal workday is from 8:15 A.M. to 5:15 P.M.

The workweek is from Monday through Friday for a total of forty (40) hours.

Variations in the hours for work may be made. Where work schedules may require it, a staggering of hours for the establishment of separate work shifts is sometimes made.

Leave of Absence

A leave of absence without pay will be considered for extraordinary circumstances not detrimental to the ministry of your department. This can be granted only at the option of the person who supervises that department and must be approved by the appropriate supervisor and the Church Administrator.

Lunch and Rest Periods

The amount of time for the lunch period is one (1) hour. A coffee break of fifteen (15) minutes in the morning and fifteen (15) minutes in the afternoon is also allowed.

Jury Duty

Employees who are required to be absent from work for jury duty will be paid the money they would have earned had they worked their normal work schedule. Any fee received for jury duty shall be turned over to the Church. If jury pay exceeds normal Church pay, the employee may keep the jury pay in excess of Church pay.

Expenses and Allowance

Expenses incurred while on Church business by any employee shall be recognized for reimbursement, if authorized in advance and approved by the appropriate authority.

Conference Attendance and Graduate Study

The Church provides a program of subsidized conference attendance and graduate study for all full-time, salaried, exempt personnel, provided that the conferences and training are related to work performed by the employee. Amount of subsidy is subject to budget provisions and approval of the Chairman of the Board or his designee. The provision does not alter hours and attendance requirements.

Exempt staff have the opportunity to enroll in graduate courses offered by colleges in the community, provided that:

A. The courses have a direct relationship to the work of the Church.

B. Only one course shall be taken at a time.

C. Approval is given by the Chairman of the Board or his designee prior to the beginning of the course.

First Christian Church will reimburse tuition for approved courses after verification of course completion has been submitted to the employee's personnel file indicating a passing grade.

Grievances

Employees are expected to discuss grievances with their immediate supervisor. If the matter cannot be settled, the grievance shall be settled by the Senior Pastor in a discussion with the employee and the employee's immediate supervisor. If the employee is then not satisfied with the settlement, the employee may present, in writing, the issue in question to the ruling board to be further reviewed.

Dismissal

Any employee may be discharged at any time for cause. No nonexempt employee will be discharged without the prior approval of the ruling board. In all cases, the employee shall be entitled to know the reasons for the dismissal.

Dress Code

In carrying out the Lord's work, you will likely come into contact with many visitors, parents of students, and members of the congregation. As your work will be under constant observation by these visitors, it is necessary to present as favorable an appearance as possible. You are requested to dress appropriately at all times in light of Whom we represent.

You should be well-groomed, presenting a favorable appearance that is appropriate to the service you are providing.

Voluntary Employment

Employment at First Christian Church of Lake City is voluntary, and at-will. This means that the employee is free to leave the Church's employment at any time by giving reasonable notice, and the Church is free to discharge the employee at any time by giving reasonable notice.

Code of Conduct

First Christian Church of Lake City is an evangelical church. It bases its teachings and guidelines for lifestyle and work ethics on the teachings found in the New Testament Scriptures. We expect the employee's conduct, on the job as well as off the job, to be in line with the moral, spiritual, and ethical guidelines of the Scriptures.

Violations of these principles can result in termination of employment.

Sexual Harassment

The Church will not allow any form of sexual harassment within the work environment. Sexual harassment as defined in this policy includes, but is not limited to, sexual advances, verbal or physical conduct of a sexual nature, visual forms of a sexual nature (e.g., signs, posters, and the like), or requests for sexual favors that

1. Interfere with work performance
2. Create an intimidating, hostile, or offensive work environment
3. Influence or tend to affect the career, salary, working conditions, responsibilities, duties, or other aspects of career development of an employee or prospective employee
4. Are an explicit or implicit condition of an individual's employment

An incidence of sexual harassment should be reported to the employee's immediate supervisor or, if the behavior involves the supervisor, to the next person in authority over the supervisor.

Job Descriptions

Each staff person should have a written job description outlining his or her basic responsibilities and duties. The personnel committee should be the group that identifies the positions and prepares the position profiles. The importance of job descriptions cannot be overemphasized. An employee has the right to know what is expected of him regarding his job duties, where he fits on the organization chart, and who, if anyone, he is supposed to supervise.

The content of the job description will depend for the most part on the specific job itself. First and foremost, the description should focus on the job position and not on the individual filling the job. Job descriptions should also be somewhat flexible. Conditions and circumstances change, and, therefore, the job description should change as well. It is a standard or guide—not rules set in stone.

The job description is also a valuable tool in evaluating employees. This subject will be dealt with later in this chapter.

The following is a sample list of church job descriptions. For the sake of flexibility and the need to be applicable across a broad range of church sizes and staffing situations, specific, individual duties have been omitted.

Senior Pastor

Responsible for all activities of the church. Responsibilities regularly include conducting services, making visitations, performing special ceremonies (such as weddings or funerals), counseling, leading business meetings, and overseeing the work of other church staff members.

Executive Pastor

Shares the responsibility for church activities with, and is responsible to, the senior pastor. Typically manages the professional staff on behalf of or in the absence of the senior pastor. On occasion acts as liaison with the lay leadership of the church. May be called upon to assist in all church functions or assigned specific areas of responsibility.

Assistant Pastor

Assists in one or more church ministries as delegated by the senior or executive pastor. May be assigned a specific area or called upon to serve in all areas.

Pastor to Singles

Responsible for the functions related to a singles ministry. Plans and directs meetings, outings, and special occasions. Counsels singles and trains leaders as needed.

Pastor/Director of Children's Ministries

Responsible for the functions related to children, usually focusing on grade-school-age children. Plans and directs activities, trains teachers, purchases supplies, and meets with parents for counseling.

Pastor of Care and Growth

Responsible for those areas related to pastoral care, which include but are not limited to visitation, weddings, and funerals. Provides oversight to volunteers involved in church visitation.

Pastor of Missions and Outreach

Directs, administers, and coordinates missions and outreach programs to integrate into each member and regular attender a mind-set for ministry and outreach beyond church family. Provides leadership by effectively managing the ministries of missions, community outreach, and evangelism. Develops and maintains "world Christian" perspective among members. Develops special programs of outreach. Assists minister of music in developing and maintaining the medium of music as an evangelistic outreach to the community.

Youth Director

Responsible for the functions related to youth, which are typically junior and senior high school age. Plans and directs activities, outings, special occasions, and youth worship services. Counsels youth and trains helpers as needed.

Christian Education Director

Responsible for planning and implementing the Christian education program, usually focusing on birth through grade-school-age children. Establishes curriculum, trains teachers, purchases supplies, and meets with parents for counseling. Attends seminars. May also include responsibility for youth and adults where appropriate for coordination.

Minister of Music

Responsible for the music activities of the church. Establishes choirs, selects and trains choir members, and selects music. Works with senior pastor in programming for regular and special church services. Typically responsible to lead worship for church services. Responsible to obtain organist and piano accompanist. Plans and conducts special music events.

196

Church Business Administrator

Responsible for the business activities of the church. Has oversight for operations, general office, finance, properties, and insurance. Establishes personnel and operations policies. Responsible for administrative records.

Organist/Pianist

Responsible for playing for any or all worship services, weddings, memorial services, funerals, choir rehearsals, and performances/concerts. Works for, or closely with, the minister of music. May be part of worship committee to plan worship services.

Sound Technician

Responsible for set-up and maintenance of all sound and duplicating equipment during scheduled activities.

Secretary—Junior

Performs routine secretarial duties. May take and transcribe dictation. Types letters and reports, answers phone, makes appointments, files documents. This is the lowest secretarial level.

Secretary—Senior

Performs moderately complex secretarial duties for senior-level manager or executive. Typically takes and transcribes dictation. Sets up and administers filing systems, types normal and confidential documents, prepares reports, arranges meetings and appointment schedules, receives and answers mail, provides direction to lower-level clerical employees, and assists in developing office policies and procedures. This is the highest secretarial level below the executive secretary.

Receptionist

Receives and greets callers and directs them to appropriate department. Operates a switchboard by receiving and placing local and long-distance calls. Performs typing and other clerical work as directed.

Janitor

Cleans and maintains buildings and offices by sweeping, dusting, polishing, scrubbing, mopping, and waxing. Removes trash, cleans furniture, washes windows, waxes and buffs floors, cleans carpets, and performs other necessary maintenance to keep the facilities clean and orderly.

Groundskeeper/Gardener/General Maintenance

Responsible for maintenance of property grounds and equipment, including mowing, watering, and replacement. May be under the supervision of the building maintenance senior or supervisor.

Preschool Director

Teaches preschool children, supervises teachers, schedules school activities and field trips, schedules employees, and may perform some bookkeeping functions.

Early Childhood Coordinator

Oversees preschool and nursery/toddler programs. Assists children's pastor in recruiting preschool teachers and leaders. Offers ongoing training, support, and discipleship of preschool teachers. Supervises preschool assistant and nursery/toddler staff. Attends weekly and monthly staff and committee meetings. Evaluates ongoing programs and strategies for improvement. Orders and oversees curriculum, equipment, and supplies, and oversees facility care and maintenance.

Elementary Teacher

Teaches children in elementary classes, does lesson plans, prepares bulletin board, coordinates field trips, leads class in light singing, and handles light telephone responsibilities.

High School Teacher

Gives specialized teaching in a given subject area and teaches in a secondary area. Responsibilities include, but are not limited to, lesson plans, extracurricular activities, counseling, and serving on departmental committees.

School Principal

The school principal is responsible for overall administration of the school. The areas of responsibility include, but are not limited to, the development of policies and the oversight of office administration, teachers, curriculum, student discipline, finance, and other duties as directed by the proper ruling body.[26]

A blank job description form (Exhibit 15–1) is provided at the end of this chapter. The sample form is a model for a medium to large church, although it can be adapted for a smaller organization.

Evaluating the Staff

One area that seems to cause some disagreement in churches has to do with the reviewing of employee performance, especially when it relates to pastoral staff. Without going into the arguments on both sides of the issue, it has been shown that some sort of ongoing and adequate staff evaluation from top to bottom will yield positive results. There are two main points to keep in mind here: accountability and effectiveness.

26. "Ministry Salary Survey," Christian Management Association, Diamond Bar, Calif., 1991.

At the risk of appearing as though the church is being run like a secular corporation, there are certain aspects of corporate practice that could certainly be implemented in the local church. Simply stated, it is neither good stewardship nor common sense to simply give church employees raises every year, especially merit increases above a Cost of Living Adjustment (COLA), without some tie-in to effectiveness. On the other hand, if a church does correlate raises to performance, how is that done? You wouldn't want to link the pastor's salary to the number of baptisms or the bookkeeper's paycheck to positive cash flow!

By way of principle, church leaders should certainly have an understanding and grasp of what they can expect from their staff. On the other hand, the church staff deserves certain courtesies from their employer—the church. While not even pretending to be exhaustive, the following guidelines offer a philosophy or overview of how church leaders should view their staff.

1. *The principle of work assignments commensurate to capacity and interest.* Every employee's potential should be given consideration in determining the tasks for which his talents may be given their highest and best use.

2. *The principle of appreciation for work well done.* Employees must be made to feel worthwhile and related to the total task. The particular contribution of an employee can be very significant if he knows that the assigned task is truly appreciated and is in the spectrum of the goals of the church.

3. *The principle of a fair day's pay for a fair day's work.* Although it has been demonstrated that employees are not motivated solely by financial incentives, "fair wages" are still quite important. If wages or salaries are considered inadequate or unfair, they do indeed become of first importance to the employee, affecting his individual achievement as well as the group effort.

4. *The principle of rewards earned, not given.* "A laborer is worthy of his wages." The opportunity to earn an advance is a highly important source of job satisfaction for most employees. A paternalistic approach of "giving" a raise, or "giving" a holiday with pay, can appear condescending and contribute to negative attitudes.

5. *The principle of fairness and consistent treatment of all employees.* One of the quickest ways to lose the respect of subordinates and to lower the morale of the work group is inconsistency in day-to-day policy and partiality in treatment of one person over another.[27]

Staff evaluations are an excellent tool to determine whether employment policies are fair, job descriptions are accurate, and the staff is working effectively and up to expectations. This process doesn't need to be complicated, intimidating, or exhaustive. The exhibits at the close of this chapter are samples of forms for staff evaluations. Exhibit 15–2 is commercially available and is suitable for use in a church setting.

27. Adapted from Robert N. Gray, *Managing the Church*, National Institute of Church Management (New York: NCC Publication Service, 1977).

Again, an employee performance review is a valuable tool in determining mutual responsibilities, expectations, and proper job fit. In my opinion, a staff member is done a disservice when the reviewer consistently gives a maximum score on the evaluation. Aside from the obvious fact that no one is perfect and everyone has room to grow, it also tells a lot about the manager style and perhaps the desire of the manager to be liked and popular. For a performance review to be effective, there must be honesty and objectivity.

To sum up, the managing of human resources—people—in the context of the local church needs to be done with care, concern, and a desire to do what is right. Personnel policies and performance evaluations need to be firm but fair. The entire matter of proper stewardship permeates this issue. Since a great deal of the church's resources is spent in this area, there is—before God—a considerable responsibility.

Many of these dedicated people have either given up more lucrative opportunities in secular fields or they have simply chosen to work at a church out of a desire to advance Christ's kingdom. Whatever the motivation, the church should set an example to reward these workers who are worthy of hire.

Exhibit 15–1
Job Description Form

FAITH EVANGELICAL CHURCH SUPPORT STAFF
Job Description

Job Title:
Department:

Job Relationships:
   Supervised by:
   Supervises:

POSITION SUMMARY:

DUTIES & RESPONSIBILITIES:

QUALIFICATIONS:
Education & experience:

Knowledge, skills and abilities:

Working conditions:

Exhibit 15–2
Employee Performance Evaluation Form

EMPLOYEE PERFORMANCE EVALUATION

Name _____ Date_____

Dept. _____ Job Title_____

Check one:　☐ Annual　☐ New Employee　☐ Termination　☐ Other _____

Date of Last Review:_____ Date Employee Began Present Position: _____
Next Scheduled Review: _____

See rating information (Part III) on reverse side of this form.	U	F	S	G	E	Comments
1. **Job Understanding:** Employee possesses a clear knowledge of the responsibilities and the task he or she must perform.						
2. **Job Performance:** The neatness, thoroughness and accuracy of employee's work.						
3. **Job Productivity:** The quality of the employee's work in terms of volume and accomplishments.						
4. **Dependability:** Can you rely upon this individual in terms of being on time and completion of tasks.						
5. **Cooperation:** The ability to work willingly with associates, subordinates, supervisors and others.						
6. **Overall Rating**						

7. General comments as to employee's strengths, weaknesses and action taken to improve job performance _____

_____

_____

_____

_____

Supervisor_____ Reviewing Officer_____

Date _____ Date_____

Has this report been discussed with employee?　☐ Yes
　　　　　　　　　　　　　　　　　　　　　　　☐ No, if not why? _____

　　　　　　　　　　　　　　　　　　　　　　　_____

　　　　　　　　　　　　　　　　　　　　　　　☐ If yes, note employee's comments _____

　　　　　　　　　　　　　　　　　　　　　　　_____

_____ Date Reviewed with Employee _____
Employee's Signature

202

Chapter 16

Worthy Is the Pastor

A recent study points out that the average American pastor with a congregation of three hundred people earns a salary of $17,875.[28] One out of five ministers moonlights to supplement his income. In fact, one study done in 1982 indicated that only 5 percent of American ministers earn more than $22,000 a year, and 14 percent earn less than $10,000.[29]

Low pay for the pastor isn't a new problem. But out of necessity many church governing boards are just now beginning to acknowledge it.

Inadequate income does produce consequences. A pastor who is concerned about providing the basic needs of his own family may not have the emotional energy to concentrate on the needs of his church. Financial burdens may contribute to a lack of enthusiasm, a low self-esteem, and a negative attitude toward the ministry. Ultimately, that will harm the congregation.

The salary pinch is no respecter of age. Many seminary graduates are forced to leave their first pastorate because they cannot support their families at an adequate standard of living. Meanwhile, combined low pay and substandard retirement programs cause some veteran pastors to stay in the ministry long after they should retire. Their fraying health and vigor hurt both themselves and the church.

The apostle Paul wrote to Timothy, "The elders who rule well are to be considered worthy of double honor, especially those who work hard at preaching and teaching. For the Scripture says, 'You shall not muzzle the ox while he is threshing,' and 'The laborer is worthy of his wages'" (1 Timothy 5:17–18).

The phrase "worthy of double honor" does not mean two pats on the back followed by a rousing rendition of "For He's a Jolly Good Fellow." If financial support of "honor" is provided to the worthy widow (5:3), then a double dose is certainly due to

28. Compensation Survey, The National Association of Church Business Administration, Fort Worth, Tex., 1991, p. 152.
29. Brochure published by Presbyterian Minister's Life Insurance Co., 1982.

the man who is her pastor. The context of 1 Timothy 5:17–18 demands that, just as one provides an ongoing reward for the work of an animal, so also should a pastor be adequately compensated for his labor.

The Bible also exhorts us to "appreciate those who diligently labor among you, and have charge over you" (1 Thessalonians 5:12). The phrase "have charge over you" literally means "stand before you." This is best illustrated by a father standing before his family (1 Timothy 3:5); it denotes responsibility, duty, and accountability.

The passage continues: "Esteem them very highly in love because of their work" (1 Thessalonians 5:13). The love mentioned here may well manifest itself through compassionate care, concern, and generosity when it comes time for the annual salary review.

Just as the business community requires an evaluation of anyone in a position of responsibility, so should the church board. (See "Evaluations" in chapter 18.) Any pay increase less than the cost of living rate for the previous twelve months should not be considered a raise. On the other hand, keep in mind the local economy, business climate, and financial condition of the church.

A good rule of thumb is to pay the senior pastor the average wage of the church ruling board. Simply ask each leader to submit figures showing his salary plus the value of his benefits. Then add the totals and divide the sum by the number of men participating.

In some situations, outside employment may be a feasible option for supplementing a low salary. Especially in smaller churches, the pastor should be given the freedom to pursue a second job without fear of stigma. Even the apostle Paul worked as a tent maker to avoid placing a financial burden on his local church.

Before allowing the pastor to take that step, however, the church board must honestly determine if they have the resources to assume his full and adequate support. Sometimes a congregation has more resources than it realizes.

In creating a compensation package, leaders should make every attempt to stretch the dollars as far as they will go. A straight salary isn't the only avenue to explore. With just a little imagination, both the minister and the congregation can benefit.

- *Reimbursement*. The congregation should pay for what it costs to have a pastor. This may involve a car allowance, professional dues, traveling expenses, meals away from home—in other words, the same costs most businesses provide.

- *Benefits*. Any fair compensation package will include health and life insurance. Disability coverage may be added. And a good pension plan should also be provided. All benefits should be furnished to the minister at no cost, thereby allowing him additional tax-free income.

- *Housing*. If the church does not provide a parsonage, a stated housing allowance over and above the pastor's salary should be given. By giving him the opportunity to buy his own home, the congregation helps him build an equity for his future. It is wise to implement the counsel of a church member who knows tax laws. Among other provisions, the Manse Allowance entitlement can be quite beneficial in handling federal taxes and saving taxable dollars.

- *Salary.* Setting a fair salary is the most difficult part of establishing an equitable pay package. A small group of trusted men should consult the pastor, discussing his needs openly, honestly, and lovingly. Future discussion or debate should also be limited to a small group situation.

Many congregations today make a big mistake in committing funds to buildings and programs rather than to people. God does not cause growth through bigger buildings or more programs but through highly motivated individuals who are loved and appreciated by their people. Faithfulness to God's Word and the effective labors of His servants are the keys to growth. Resources should be directed at people first, then programs and facilities.

"Let the church keep the pastor poor and God can keep him humble" is a faulty motto. Most men serving in pulpits today are highly trained, with the majority possessing advanced degrees. In obedience to God, a congregation should pay a minister what he is worth. And God can still keep him humble.

Chapter 17

Matters of Conscience

Opting Out of the Social Security System

I certify that I am conscientiously opposed to, or because of my religious principles I am opposed to, the acceptance (for services I perform as a minister, member of religious order not under a vow of poverty or a Christian Science practitioner) of any public insurance that makes payments in the event of death, disability, old age, or retirement; or that makes payments toward the cost of, or provides services for, medical care. (Public insurance includes insurance systems established by the Social Security Act.) . . . Under penalties of perjury, I declare that I have examined this application and to the best of my knowledge and belief it is true and correct.[30]

Many ministers read this section on IRS Form 4361 when they apply to "opt out" of the Social Security system and pause—some for longer periods of time than others. Let's face it, for most pastors this option presents the proverbial "horns of a dilemma." Some ministers ask themselves, "Am I really opposed to all government assistance or just government insurance?"

The tension between staying in the Social Security system or checking out often boils down to a personal debate over the merits and the soundness of the Social Security system versus one's own opposition to receiving financial help from the government. It should be noted, however, that for some ministers this is an easy decision on moral grounds. They are simply against accepting assistance from "Caesar." The secular government in their thinking is not part of God's plan for His servants. God, they believe, through the local church, will provide for all their needs, including a retirement plan.

This would mean, of course, that based on their personal beliefs they would be opposed to FEMA disaster assistance, Medicare, SA loans, Pell Grants for their children's education, and welfare assistance for their needy church members. For

---

30. See IRS Form 4361 (Exhibit 2–2).

example, suppose a church member who is a single mother approaches the pastor with a request for financial assistance. Would the minister refer the woman to the local welfare office? Would this be consistent with the minister's views on accepting public assistance? This issue, therefore, boils down to the question of whether a minister is conscientiously opposed to accepting all government assistance.

If opposition to federal assistance is universal and across the board, what does a minister do with the matter of accepting social security coverage as a result of secular employment, either before or after he or she entered the ministry? How can a minister on moral grounds accept social security and medicare benefits based on benefits derived from nonministerial income and yet refuse to pay social security taxes on ministerial income? Unfortunately, this is a very common practice. Granted, their social security benefits are probably somewhat reduced. However, as a result of broad ranges in the social security plan for earnings levels, it is possible for many bivocational ministers to opt out of social security payments and still receive social security benefits later in life. From a moral standpoint, this would be the same as having your cake and eating it too!

Then there are those who, although opposed to government programs, look at this issue pragmatically. First, they believe that the Social Security system will be bankrupt in ten years—which is possible. Furthermore, the 15.3 percent of their annual income paid by means of Schedule SE each year could be extra cash in their pockets. Finally, the money paid in annually could be placed in a high-quality investment portfolio and possibly produce a better retirement nest egg. Unfortunately, it doesn't always happen that way. Many ministers pocket their savings, live in a church-provided parsonage, and then retire broke.

Although the economics of "opting out" may seem attractive, that really isn't the issue. Once again it is a matter of searching your conscience instead of evaluating the economic risk and returns.

The Facts

All ministers are automatically covered by Social Security for services in the exercise of their ministry unless an exemption has been received by filing IRS Form 4361. This form includes a statement certifying that you oppose, either conscientiously or because of religious principle, the acceptance of any public insurance (with respect to services performed as a minister), including social security coverage. This includes insurance that helps pay for or provides services for medical care and includes benefits from any system established by the Social Security Act.

A person's opposition must be based on religious belief. In essence, to claim the exemption for self-employment tax, you must:

- File Form 4361 (see Exhibit 2–2)
- Be conscientiously opposed to public insurance because of your individual religious considerations (not because of your general conscience) or because the principles are shared by a religious denomination
- File for reasons mentioned above and not for personal economic benefit

Tax expert Dan Busby, CPA, cautions, "Very few ministers can legitimately sign 4361. Many ministers have signed 4361 inappropriately because they were afraid the Social Security system will fail or because they prefer to invest their own dollars themselves."[31]

However, for the sake of argument, let's assume that the decision of whether or not to remain in the program is based solely on economic aspects of the social security program. The alternative would be to provide the necessary funds to replace these benefits. How much would that cost? There are a number of factors to consider:

- *Income Replacement.* Suppose a worker retiring in 1993 had decided to use his personal savings and investments to replace the income benefit available through Social Security. Estimates suggest that a worker would need to have saved a nest egg of $400,000, currently yielding 7 percent a year to fund a program equal to today's social security benefits. The social security income benefit also has a regular cost-of-living adjustment that keeps up with inflation. That would have to be factored into the "do-it-yourself" plan too.
- *Survivor's Insurance.* If the minister dies under Social Security, funds are provided for the surviving spouse. To replace this coverage, a life insurance policy would need to be purchased—one that, unlike Social Security, would require a physical.
- *Disability Insurance.* This is another cost that would be necessary in order to assure a disability benefit. Again, the minister would have to pass the physical at his or her current age in order to qualify for a disability policy.
- *Medicare-type Insurance.* Medicare-A, the basic hospitalization benefit, would cost between $5,000 and $6,000 per year at current rates. Some ministers may be eligible for this benefit, however, if they have forty quarters of qualified employment in a secular job. Medicare-B, the major medical coverage, now costs social security recipients only $32 per month.

Remember, this is coverage that kicks in after you have retired and your employer's health plan may not be available to you. To replace it would require purchasing health insurance at age sixty-five—not an easy task.

The Bottom Line

So what would all this cost? If we figured on having enough capital to generate interest payments equivalent to social security retirement income and the cost of premiums for

31. Dan Busby, CPA, *Minister's Tax & Financial Guide*, 1994 ed. (Grand Rapids: Zondervan, 1994), 92.

survivor's insurance, disability insurance, and a major medical health plan starting at retirement age, the first year start-up cost would be close to $430,000. In addition, to hold those levels of income and insurance premiums, it would be necessary to maintain a minimum 7 percent yield on your nest egg for the rest of your life.

If you are considering filing for exemption from Social Security, consider this. Christian attorney and tax expert Richard Hammer points out, "It is possible (if not likely) that this exemption will be interpreted to exclude from any future national health care program those ministers who have opted out of Social Security. This is a very serious development, particularly in light of the unavailability of Medicare coverage for such ministers."

Although I am not a great supporter of, nor an apologist for, the Federal government, this has been an attempt to move the question of a minister opting out of this program back to the real issue and to remove some of the arguments pushing against a minister's conscience. Here is the problem: Though Jesus says, "Render to Caesar the things that are Caesar's" (Matthew 22:21), Caesar, in this case, is giving you an option. However, you cannot file for exemption for economic reasons. So the options must include your religious convictions, which should have some sort of scriptural justification.

Furthermore, you must inform the ordaining, commissioning, or licensing body of your church that you are opting out of Social Security because you are opposed to public insurance. So, as you can see, although it's a matter of religious consideration, it is not necessarily a private position that you can keep to yourself. Above all, it is not an economic decision. Therefore, it is a matter of conscience and not cash!

Making Loans to Clergy

A frequent obstacle to hiring a new pastor is the issue of affordable housing. Many areas of the country have high housing costs. For a minister moving from a rural setting, this can present a rather difficult complication—especially if the pastor's current salary is based on a lower geographic housing expense. (Housing expense is not an issue when there is a church-provided parsonage.)

- *Possible solution*: Some churches make a loan to their pastors to assist them in the purchase of a home. The church often charges a very low rate of interest and some churches waive the interest completely. The problem is that these loans can create tax consequences for the pastor and paperwork headaches for the church.
- *Before a loan is made*: Find out if your state permits a loan of any kind to an employee of the church. A number of states prohibit any loans by a nonprofit organization to its employees, whether interest is charged or not. The 1994 Congress came close to enacting legislation under which any loans by a nonprofit organization to an employee would be subject to significant penalties. Although the provision did not

pass, it will likely be reintroduced. Such a law would probably be applied only on a prospective basis.

- *More caution*: Even under current law, no-interest or below-market loans to a minister may be considered as "private inurement" of the church's income. This means that the IRS could take the position that a church is using tax-exempt funds for non-tax-exempt purposes. The good news is that the IRS generally does not raise this issue except on loans of a significant size.

- *Reporting requirements*: If a no-interest or low-interest loan to a pastor is for $10,000 or more, the church is obligated for certain reporting. The church must compute the difference between the interest rate charged on the loan and a standard interest rate (as defined monthly by the IRS). This difference in interest rates (called "forgone interest") must be reported as additional income on Form W-2 or 1099-MISC. The type of reporting form used depends on whether the church considers the minister an employee (W-2) or self-employed (1099-MISC) for income purposes.

  If the loan is structured as a demand note, the forgone interest is computed on an annual basis. However, if the loan is a term loan, the forgone interest is computed for the entire term of the loan and added to the minister's compensation on the date the loan is made.

  Even no- or low-interest loans of less than $10,000 create forgone interest income that should be added to the minister's income. The reporting by the church to the IRS for these smaller loans is simply not required by law.

- *Forgiving loans*: If a church chooses to forgive any portion of the interest or principal on a loan (whether at full interest or principal, or not), the amount forgiven must be reported as additional compensation on Form W-2 or 1099-MISC.

- *Impact of itemizing deductions*: Ministers who get a loan to help provide their own home generally can itemize in Schedule A (because of real estate tax and mortgage interest) instead of using the standard deduction. If the loan is recorded, the interest expense is deductible on Schedule A and, therefore, is a "wash" against forgone interest income. The interest expense is also includible as housing expense if the loan proceeds are used for housing.

To sum up, if a church desires to make a loan to a pastor for housing or any other purpose, the first step is to determine whether the proposed loan is legal in your state. If it is not legal, the loan should not be made. If a low- or no-interest loan of more than $10,000 is made, the church must fulfill its duty to compute and report additional income on the forms filed with the IRS.

Chapter 18

Toward a Higher Standard

The term *professional* is tossed about a great deal today. Accusing someone of not acting "professionally" is almost unforgivable in many business circles. However, it's often difficult to define exactly what it means to be a professional. Some believe that it is simply a matter of "keeping your cool" in a stressful situation, whereas in other circles it means no more than producing work that is of a certain quality of sophistication.

Translating what secular society considers as professionalism into the environment of a multistaff church can be difficult. Church members often expect a certain level of competency and skill from their ministerial staff—and well they should. Moreover, many parishioners don't understand the culture of a church staff, and too often pastors don't appreciate what the world considers as a level of proficiency.

So how does a senior minister create a professional culture within a staff that will meet an objective standard as well as the expectations of the church members? Specifically, what does professionalism look like in a church context?

The most effective method to use when establishing proficiency in this area is to develop a set of policies or standards. These guidelines should encompass the minister's commitment and conduct.

Commitment

Each staff member, first and foremost, should understand the mission of the church. Therefore, "vision casting" is a vital and fundamental responsibility of the senior pastor. Every staff person should be heading in the same overall direction with no "Lone Ranger" types. Staff members who believe that their gift or ministry is unique and can operate better independently of the rest of the staff are not part of the team effort. This communicates a lack of cohesiveness and unity and can set up power bases, or "turf," which in time can be disruptive.

Second, aside from the fact that a staff pastor should be a church member in good standing, there are other actions that would demonstrate devotion to the overall ministries of the church:

- Weekly attendance at one of the worship services (if multiple services exist)
- Serving in ministries that fit the pastor's gifts and relate directly to the needs of the church
- Cheerful financial support of the church ministries, using the tithe as a guideline (regular giving is not to be used to purchase goods or services for any church ministry that is not approved by the ruling leadership)
- Personal time in prayer and Bible reading at least five times each week, sharing spiritual insights with others
- Living a life of Christian love and righteousness at home and in the world, making sure that the minister's life is balanced with sufficient quality family time, as well as time to develop friendships with the lost

Conduct

Another one of the issues touching on professionalism has to do with appearance. In business, you are usually judged, among other factors, by the clothes you wear. The old saying "Clothes make the man" on the surface certainly sounds materialistic, but it can still be somewhat reflective of a person's taste, opinion of themselves, and the environment in which they operate. Some "creative" or artistic organizations don't care what people wear in the workplace. Others try to develop a certain image by insisting that employees dress to a particular standard that management believes is appropriate for their industry. The operative word here is *appropriate*. It is not unreasonable to expect church employees to dress in a manner that is acceptable and in good taste.

Many churches have a policy that requires church staff to dress in "business" attire during office hours and on Sunday morning. Whereas neat, casual attire may be appropriate on some occasions, it is not the norm. Youth pastors would have the most flexibility, yet they are not to be sloppy.

One of the greatest complaints heard from church members has to do with the hours worked (or not worked!) by the staff. Often there is a perception that employees come and go as they please, with little if any accountability. Some people believe that ministers just don't work very hard. Perhaps there are instances in which some of these images are borne out in reality, but for the mainstream church of the nineties, workloads and responsibilities for the ministerial staff have become much more sophisticated and demanding. Unfortunately, much of what a pastor accomplishes is not seen by the average layperson. Nevertheless, there still needs to be some basic guidelines in order to establish a system of accountability for the benefit of the staff and church members both.

Workweek

A workweek framework should be identified. For full-time staff, a minimum of forty hours a week should be required. Some churches, except with regard to the senior pastor, exclude Sunday as a workday. The rationale is that Christians, whether they have a secular or religious job, should be giving some portion of their energies back to the Lord. It is felt that the "work" performed on Sunday is a contribution to the body of Christ and should be without compensation.

Sundays

- Responsibilities on Sunday extending beyond the regular service times are considered workweek time.
- Attendance and participation during the regular service is considered voluntary ministry and not part of the workweek hours. (This provision is greatly appreciated by lay workers.)
- Visibility and availability before and after the worship and class times are expected, but not during the worship time. Unless staff members are a part of the program, they are not to emphasize their role; instead, they are to join in the services with the rest of the members.
- Worship attendance is to be scheduled so that there are ministers present in every service.

Time Away

Absences, especially on Sundays, have the potential to spark comments about the staff's work ethic. Once again, conduct that demonstrates commitment and accountability is to be welcomed as a way to show one's concern and sensitivity on this issue. The following are suggested guidelines:

- The senior pastor must approve all time away.
- The pastor, prior to being away, is responsible to provide quality ministry in his absence.
- A maximum of seven days per year (which cannot be accrued) may be taken for personal ministry-related activities. This is especially important when a minister develops a program that is recognized outside the local congregation. Resentment can build among other staff members, as well as church attenders, when a minister is gone repeatedly in pursuit of outside interests. The leadership needs to decide how

they wish to handle external involvement on the part of a pastor, including the senior minister.

- Time away that is considered a part of church ministry responsibility is considered workweek time; expenses shall be paid for by the church and honorariums returned to the church.
- School is considered personal time and expense, unless there is an approved exception.

In order to prevent problems and misunderstandings, other issues having to do with the focus of one's ministry, outside sources of income, and other involvements should be addressed. Without trying to deal with every conceivable issue on this subject, three general areas should at least be covered in a summary fashion.

Interpersonal Relationships

Although the issue of staff unity, mutual cooperation, and respect would not normally be a policy matter, the subject of male/female relationships definitely is. This entire issue has been moved to center stage in the realm of personnel management. A church, therefore, should have a formal written policy covering what constitutes sexual harassment and the procedure for reporting such actions (see p. 194). Religious organizations are not exempt from laws in this area and must take careful steps to inform all staff members of the definition, limits, and consequences of misdeeds in this regard.

Evaluations

- The top leaders in the church should conduct a thorough annual evaluation of the senior minister.
- The senior pastor's immediate subordinates should also be reviewed by the top leadership. This will ensure objectivity and the avoidance of any "filtering" of comments through the senior minister to the leaders.

Some boards don't want to evaluate the staff pastors. So they either allow the senior pastor to handle this responsibility or they appoint a personnel committee of some sort to handle the reviews. The point is, performance evaluations should be done on an annual basis, and they should be meaningful.

There are those who believe that evaluating a minister's performance is wrong. After all, they contend, he isn't a baseball player striving for a .300 batting average or a salesman trying to meet a quota. They are correct to a degree—to try to equate effectiveness in the ministry from a quantitative standard certainly would not be fitting. (On the other hand, if the worship attendance dropped 50 percent in twelve months, the question of performance will definitely come up among the members!)

A pastor should welcome an opportunity to be evaluated. Here is an opening to invite church leaders into the world of ministry. He could share with them the long hours spent in sermon preparation, hospital visitation, counseling, administrative details, and late-night phone calls. And don't forget those emotional burdens. Officiating at the funeral of a child, counseling a distraught wife, trying to save a failing marriage, always having to be the cheerleader, the pressure to preach inspiring messages, and making those heartfelt appeals to meet the budget. This is a chance to show your leaders that shepherding is more than preaching a Sunday message. It's a golden opportunity to ask them to pray with you and for you.

A meaningful evaluation will take into consideration a pastoral staff member's effectiveness and his contribution to the church's goals. Results of the appraisal should be shared personally with the pastor to help him recognize his strengths as well as weaknesses. These checkpoints could be used as a starting point:

- *Responsibility*—the number of people under his supervision and the number to whom he ministers
- *Replaceability*—the degree of difficulty in replacing the pastor
- *Teamwork*—the degree of interacting with, contributing to, and mutually supporting other ministries
- *Quality*—the degree of effectiveness in: (1) discipleship and leadership development; (2) evangelism, edification, and equipping; (3) creativity and innovation; (4) excitement, dedication, and confidence engendered in those involved
- *Qualification*—number of years on church staff, degrees, background, and experience.
- *Thrust*—the degree of significance and necessity of this specific ministry in furthering the total church ministry

A grade-point system (e.g., 1–5, with 5 being the best) may offer the best means of "grading" the individual. A multiple pastoral staff sample evaluation form is provided at the end of this chapter; see Exhibit 18–1 (Pastoral Impact Effectiveness Sheet). Exhibit 18–2 (Ministry Profile Form) would be suitable for a more in-depth evaluation of professional staff. The staff person completes the form, and the leader, department head, or other person in authority reviews the results. The information is then compared to the individual's job description or the expectations of the church board as it relates to this person's job performance.

One additional factor could also be considered. In the expression "especially those who work hard" (1 Timothy 5:17), the phrase "work hard" comes from the Greek word *kopiaō*, which means "to work hard, toil, labor, strive, struggle; become tired, grow weary."

I believe that a "sweat factor" should be considered in an evaluation. Those churches that have multiple staffs, with individuals carrying various loads of responsibility, need to account for this extra effort. The "up front" leaders are not necessarily the most important. Associate pastors dealing with counseling situations, for example, may carry a load just as heavy as senior pastors.

The point here is that professionalism is encouraged when there are certain directly related performance standards set in place. Furthermore, to reward only the minister who has the public ministry is a mistake. Many secular businesses understand the importance of recognizing every employee. For instance, how many times have you seen an "Employee of the Month" in a fast-food restaurant, a hotel, or hospital? If you will notice, the employee of the month is never the store, restaurant, or hotel manager. A church staff that understands the importance and significance of the evaluation process as well as what is expected of them will, in most cases, respond positively to standards of commitment and conduct.

Outside Income

Books, lecture materials, articles, and outlines are the personal property of the writer; royalties belong to the author, not the church. It should be made clear, however, how much time can be spent writing for outside publication, especially if it involves time during the workweek. Many professionals coming out of academic settings assume that time spent writing is part of their job. It's the "publish or perish" concept. That's why a clear policy in this area should be established. Authorship should be encouraged, but not to the detriment of the ministry. Furthermore, a guideline should be stated regarding the use of a church secretary to work on projects from which the minister receives a royalty.

Perhaps it would be best if the minister provided a report of outside income on an annual basis to establish a level of accountability in this area.

Nonministry Obligations

The matter of outside board involvement, establishing ministries separate from the church, or acting as a conservator or executor of an estate should all be approved by the board of directors of the church. Accusations of conflict of interest or a lack of commitment could arise from these types of extracurricular activities. Everything should be up front and out in the open.

There are executives or managers in the congregation who would look at these guidelines and see nothing wrong with them. In their opinion, they are reasonable and demonstrate an appreciation for accountability. There are, on the other hand, many ministers who would balk at these "rules," feeling that their ministry style is being hindered.

The issue here is one of proper appearances, conduct, and devotion on the part of the ministerial staff. The New Testament speaks of church members bestowing honor on those who "diligently labor among you, and have charge over you" (1 Thessalonians 5:12). *Receiving* honor versus *deserving* honor may be the real issue.

218

Conclusion

Proficient, diligent, and effective? Professionalism or the perception of it in some organizations may be created with an M.B.A., a pin-striped suit, or a cellular phone! But that's not how it works in the kingdom of God. We need a different benchmark . . . a higher standard. The opinion our church members have of the staff needs to be rooted in commitment and conduct. The manner in which these activities directly relate to the ministries of the church is the way your staff demonstrates professionalism.

In the final analysis, though, it is the motive behind our efforts that really counts. Our labors should not be viewed only as a witness to those around us but, more importantly, as an offering to God, which represents a gift of love to Him.

Exhibit 18–1
Pastoral Impact Effectiveness Sheet
Grace Community Church

Please write in the appropriate number of 1 to 5
(Minimal or Weak — 1 2 3 4 5 — Maximal or Strong)

NAME	IMPACT FACTORS 0	1	2	3	4	5	Ttl.	NAME	IMPACT FACTORS 0	1	2	3	4	5	Ttl.

PASTORAL IMPACT FACTORS   CONSIDERATIONS

1	RESPONSIBILITY	The number of people involved in leadership & ministry, & the number of people directly & significantly influenced by this ministry..
2	REPLACEABILITY	The degree of difficulty in replacing this person in this ministry..
3	TEAM	The degree of interfacing, contributing to and mutually supporting other ministries at Grace..
4	QUALITY	The degree of effectiveness in the following: discipleship and leadership development; evangelization, edification & equipping; creativity & innovation; excitement, dedication & confidence engendered in those involved..
5	THRUST	The degree of significance & necessity this ministry has on the thrust of Grace Church specifically & the Kingdom in general..
0	THE COMBINED WEIGHT	given to years on Grace staff, degrees, background & experience. . .

220

Exhibit 18–2
Ministry Profile Form

MINISTRY PROFILE

==

Below, list any special goals or projects
currently being worked on, over and above
normal responsibilities. (Such as articles
being written, curriculum, studies, etc.)

Special comments

==

1.

_____

2.

_____

3.

_____

4.

_____

5.

_____

6.

_____